Induction and Example

Induction and Example

A Rhetorical Exegesis in the Letter of Galatians

C. T. Johnson

Foreword by Troy W. Martin

☙PICKWICK *Publications* • Eugene, Oregon

INDUCTION AND EXAMPLE
A Rhetorical Exegesis in the Letter of Galatians

Copyright © 2022 C. T. Johnson. All rights reserved. Except for brief quotations in critical publications or reviews, no part of this book may be reproduced in any manner without prior written permission from the publisher. Write: Permissions, Wipf and Stock Publishers, 199 W. 8th Ave., Suite 3, Eugene, OR 97401.

Pickwick Publications
An Imprint of Wipf and Stock Publishers
199 W. 8th Ave., Suite 3
Eugene, OR 97401

www.wipfandstock.com

PAPERBACK ISBN: 978-1-6667-3377-8
HARDCOVER ISBN: 978-1-6667-2870-5
EBOOK ISBN: 978-1-6667-2871-2

Cataloguing-in-Publication data:

Names: Johnson, C. T., author. | Martin, Troy W., foreword.

Title: Induction and example : a rhetorical exegesis in the letter of Galatians. / by C. T. Johnson; foreword by Troy W. Martin.

Description: Eugene, OR: Pickwick Publications, 2020 | Includes bibliographical references and index.

Identifiers: ISBN 978-1-6667-3377-8 (paperback) | ISBN 978-1-6667-2870-5 (hardcover) | ISBN 978-1-6667-2871-2 (ebook)

Subjects: LCSH: Bible. Galatians—Language, style. | Rhetoric in the Bible. | Rhetoric, Ancient. | Aristotle.

Classification: BS2685.2 J64 2022 (print) | BS2685.2 (ebook)

08/09/22

Contents

Foreword by Troy W. Martin | ix

1. **Introduction to Aristotle** | 1
   Principles of Induction | 2
   Summary | 6

2. **Aristotle's Example (Gk. *Paradeigma*)** | 8
   The Distinction between Aristotle's
      Induction and Example | 9
   Aristotle's Entechnic Proofs | 11
   Aristotle's Historical Example | 13
   Aristotle's Example: Part to Whole to Part | 16
   Deliberative Examples in Oratorical Speeches | 17
   Comprehension and Persuasiveness of Examples | 19
   Summary | 20

3. **Induction: Observation and Experience** | 21
   Observation | 22
   Interpreting Biblical Observation | 23
   Experience | 27
   The Experience of the Theologian and the Lay Person | 28

Interpreting Biblical Experience | 29
　　High and Low Probabilities | 35
　　Summary | 37

4. **Identifying Biblical Example** | 38
　　The Contextual Example | 41
　　The Historical Example | 41
　　Discovery of Historical Examples | 45
　　Reinterpreting the Historical Example | 50
　　Recent or Present Examples | 52
　　Personal Example | 57
　　The Analogy | 62
　　Summary | 65

5. **Galatians: Arguing the Causa/Stasis** | 66
　　Analysis of Paul's Sub-Issues | 69
　　An Analysis and Function of Paul's Examples in Gal 1–2 | 70
　　Paul's Inductive Experience and Paul's
　　　　Inductive Theology | 76
　　The Galatians' Inductive Experience | 81
　　Summary | 84

6. **Paul's Inductive Examples** | 85
　　Example One: The Testimony of the Judean
　　　　Churches (Gal 1:21–24) | 88
　　Example Two: The Jerusalem Event (Gal 2:1–10) | 92
　　Example Three: The Antiochian Event (Gal 2:11–14) | 99
　　Example Four: The Faith of Abraham (Gal 3:6–9) | 110

Conclusion | 119

Appendix: A Brief Survey of the Scholarship
on Aristotle's First Principles | 121
　　Sense Perception | 122
　　Observation | 129
　　Particular Objects | 130
　　Particulars and Universals | 131
　　Memory | 133
　　Recollection | 135

Experience | 137
A Brief Survey on Nous | 140
Aristotle's Universals | 142
The Ability to Explain Universals | 144

Bibliography | 147
Ancient Documents Index | 157

Foreword

FROM THE EARLIEST BEGINNINGS of rhetorical studies, discussions and investigations of rhetorical example lag far behind treatments of other areas of rhetoric. Aristotle discusses rhetorical example or the paradigm along with the enthymeme as the two means of logical argumentation but then focuses on the enthymeme and treats the paradigm only briefly.[1] His treatment consists of distinguishing between the two and then describing two species of paradigms, the historical and the invented. He concludes his brief treatment of paradigms with a few remarks about when to use them. Other ancient rhetoricians such as Anaximenes of Lampsacus, Cicero, Quintilian, and the author of the *Rhetorica ad Herennium* likewise provide only brief explanations of the paradigm or exemplum. Their inadequate and incomplete treatments of rhetorical example reflect their mental conceptions that it provides only supporting testimony, amplification, embellishment, or vividness to explicit enthymematic arguments and is therefore of less importance.[2]

---

1. Martin, "Invention and Arrangement," 100.
2. Anderson, *Glossary of Greek Rhetorical Terms*, 87–88.

Foreword

The trend set by these ancient rhetoricians continues into modern rhetorical studies. In his rhetorical dictionary, for example, David E. Aune devotes eight pages to the enthymeme but only a quarter page to the example.[3] My own survey of Pauline rhetorical studies found several studies devoted specifically to Paul's enthymematic argumentation but only a few focused on his exemplary or paradigmatic argumentation.[4] Pauline rhetorical studies tend to treat rhetorical examples on an ad hoc basis as they arise in Paul's letters and largely identify and differentiate these examples by the persons Paul uses to construct his examples.[5] Thus, these studies identify Paul's use of the examples of Christ, Timothy, Epaphroditus, Israel personified, and of course himself but nevertheless assign a moral function to all these examples. The restriction of so many different paradigms in Paul's argumentation to a single function leaves some lingering issues about Paul's use of inductive argumentation. Perhaps other types of paradigms and other functions of the paradigm remain to be discovered in Paul's letters or perhaps the ancient rhetorical notion of rhetorical example has been either inappropriately or inadequately applied to Paul's rhetoric.[6] I conclude my survey of example in Pauline rhetorical studies by noting, "These lingering issues indicate that . . . more work is needed on the paradigm to assess adequately its role in Paul's logical argumentation."[7]

Johnson begins his study by acknowledging the disproportionate scholarly attention given to deductive argumentation and the enthymeme and the relative disparagement of inductive reasoning generally and particularly of rhetorical example. He then proceeds to a thorough examination of Aristotle's description of the essence and function of example. Unlike previous studies that focus only on what Aristotle says, however, Johnson begins

---

3. Aune, *Westminster Dictionary of New Testament and Early Christian Literature and Rhetoric*, 150–57, 173.
4. Martin, "Invention and Arrangement," 94–102.
5. Martin, "Invention and Arrangement," 100–102.
6. Anderson, *Ancient Rhetorical Theory and Paul*, 223.
7. Martin, "Invention and Arrangement," 102.

Foreword

by investigating Aristotle's conception of induction as part of his total philosophical agenda informed and driven by an empirical method. Johnson demonstrates that induction is neither anterior nor inferior to deduction but rather comes first in the process of knowledge formation since inductive discovery provides the empirical data for generalizations and universals from which deductive reasoning proceeds. Johnson also notes that induction seeks more than inference and generalities by seeking to discover the nature of things, and he explores the importance of this type of reasoning for inductive theology. He demonstrates that much of New Testament theological reflection begins with sense perception, observation, and experience and then proceeds through inductive reasoning to theological claims about God, Christ, humans, sin, and salvation. This important part of Johnson's book will be particularly interesting to New Testament theologians.

By elevating the importance of inductive reasoning, Johnson also enhances the importance of example in rhetorical argumentation and devotes the remainder of his study to a description not only of the essence of example but of the various ways examples contribute to rhetorical argumentation. Rather than simply equating induction and example as many studies are prone to do, Johnson distinguishes induction as a logical technique designed to construct a rational argument from example as a rhetorical technique designed to persuade. Although example is a type of induction, context becomes much more important for the selection and shaping of rhetorical example than for non-rhetorical types of inductive reasoning. According to Johnson, a rhetorical example depends on its immediate and larger context for its meaning, interpretation, and function in the larger argument. Johnson thus offers a welcome corrective to those studies that decontextualize rhetorical examples by analyzing them as self-contained arguments largely independent from their larger argumentative context.

Johnson illustrates his understanding of rhetorical examples by investigating their purpose and function in several New Testament passages before turning to his primary goal of analyzing four paradeigmata or exempla in Paul's Letter to the Galatians. Johnson first discusses Paul's overall rhetorical argument in Galatians and identifies the causa as a defense of the truth of Paul's gospel against the circumcision gospel of the agitators. Rather than serving a moral purpose, these examples, according to Johnson argue this causa by demonstrating the truth of the gospel. The example of the testimony of the Judean churches (Gal 1:21–24) that Paul's conversion was genuine implies by analogy that his gospel is as well. The example of the Jerusalem event (Gal 2:1–10) emphasizes Paul's acceptance by the pillars of the church and infers that his gospel was accepted as well. The example of the Antiochian event (Gal 2:11–14) portrays Paul in defense of the true gospel and implies that he is doing the same in the Galatian controversy. The example of the Faith of Abraham (Gal 3:6–9) argues the causa by portraying Abraham's justification by faith before he was circumcised and thus aligning him with Paul's gospel rather than with the circumcision gospel of the agitators. According to Johnson, all these examples establish through inductive reasoning the universal principle of the truth of the gospel.

Johnson's work is one of the most sustained, nuanced, and helpful studies of rhetorical example to appear in the field of New Testament Rhetorical Criticism, and it provides some remedy for the relative neglect of this area of ancient and early Christian rhetoric. Even those who do not agree with his exegetical assumptions or conclusions will profit from his careful investigation of rhetorical example and especially his extensive explanation of paradeigma and induction in Aristotle's rhetorical and philosophical treatises. Johnson concludes that "example is ubiquitous in the biblical corpus appearing in various forms namely, historical examples, present examples, personal examples, and analogy," but he helps bring this ubiquity into sharper focus, and I welcome the publication of his work.

    Troy W. Martin
    Professor of Bible
    Saint Xavier University
    Chicago, IL

1

Introduction to Aristotle

ARISTOTLE IS WIDELY KNOWN in the Ancient and Western world for his work on inductive reasoning. Admittedly his philosophy on induction is related either directly or indirectly with every major treatise and theory attributed to him, and therefore it is virtually impossible to grasp other subjects without first considering and knowing it. Three concepts that are contingent on Aristotle's induction: his first principles, the rhetorical example, and deductive arguments.[1] Marc Gasser Wingate states, "We learn [Aristotle's] first principles by induction (ἐπαγωγῇ), a form of cognitive development that begins with perception and progresses through a series of increasingly sophisticated states in which various universal concepts come to be formed in our souls."[2] Aristotle's induction also forms an argument by example because induction is the source material for the rhetorical proof. In other words, induction supplies the example with a generalization (or universals) and that becomes the source to argue a particular case in the present. There are two types of rhetorical examples: "arguments by analogy, called

---

1. See more on Aristotle's first principles in the appendix.
2. Wingate, "Aristotle on Induction and First Principles," 1.

Induction and Example

arguments from likeness (ὅμοιος), and arguments from example (παράδειγμα). Both these arguments produce probable or plausible conclusions."[3] Aristotle's induction is also the groundwork for deductive arguments; deduction demonstrates those inductive discoveries through syllogisms.

Principles of Induction

Unlike deduction, colloquially labeled "top-down reasoning," where the argument moves from the general to the specific and the conclusion logically follows the premises, the nature of induction, familiarly termed "bottom-up reasoning," the opposite is true, here the movement is from specific observation to the general, in which the conclusion states more than the evidence in the premises. What we have therefore is missing evidence that is outside the logical chain unaccounted for in the conclusion, a leap if you will from the premises to the conclusion. Another way to explain the leap is "we leap from a particular case or cases to all; we infer that because a certain thing is true of a certain case or cases, it is true for all cases resembling others."[4] This leap is not blind or based on dissimilar cases (or evidence), but there exists a pattern or a relationship between all such cases.

We might add, all the evidence does not have to be extant to determine what a thing is; it is not compulsory to observe or experience an object all day and every day for a year to gain insight to advance in knowledge. Induction does not need to be perfect with an exhaustive examination of the object of a particular class or kind to determine the truth of it. It would have been pointless to examine all the cows in the world to determine what a cow is or to examine every sheep to state what a sheep is. To say, "There are 'cows' is to say that these animals all share the same (essential) nature. To say 'all cows are mammals' is to do the same thing but by specifying

---

3 Groarke, *Aristotelian Account of Induction*, 19.
4. Thilly, *Process of Inductive Inference*, 30.

Introduction to Aristotle

something about what that nature is."[5] This is true for dogs and cats because their name classification and how they are defined tells us they possess certain qualities. This remains true and always will, even if a dog or cat has one eye or three legs, because these features are not essential characteristics only accidental properties. Even in Aristotle's explanation of bileless animals (man, horse, mule), he would have to seek out, observe, and inspect every bileless animal (via perfect induction) to determine that they are long lived.[6] This is highly unlikely and virtually impossible.

Since this leap or creativity is unaccounted for and, for this reason, subject to conjecture and skepticism, philosophers and logicians often cogitate—this is the problem of induction. They argue that the possibility of new information or data may counter the verity of an inductive claim. Thus, rationalists tend to cast off and devalue the utility of induction because there is always a missing link in the argumentative (logical) chain, and so inductive arguments are considered probable (or strong or weak). Bertrand Russell famously stated:

> It must be conceded, to begin with, that the fact that two things have been found often together and never apart does not, by itself, suffice to prove demonstratively that they will be found together in the next case we examine. The most we can hope is that the oftener things are found together, the more probable it becomes that they will be found together another time, and that, if they have been found together often enough, the probability will amount almost to certainty. It can never quite reach certainty, because we know that in spite of frequent repetitions there sometimes is a failure at the last, as in the case of the chicken whose neck is wrung. Thus probability is all we ought to seek.[7]

---

5. Groarke, "Jumping the Gaps," 487.

6. Groarke explains that "we can only know that 'particular long-lived [bileless] animals' ... share a certain characteristic, through an initial inspection of the individual members of that species." Groarke, *Aristotelian Account of Induction*, 118.

7. Russell, *Problems of Philosophy*, 65–66.

Induction and Example

Although Russell questions the certainty of inductive reasoning, he does contend that the greater the number of cases found together, the more assurance we will have in the event occurring again.

Let us add that "if induction cannot logically guarantee its conclusions, could it not offer an approximate take on the world?"[8] One may discover through induction the best course of action to take in the future. An ancient Greek, for example, may observe and experience that every time Aristotle lectures on rhetoric in the streets of Athens, he attracts an enormous crowd, making it difficult to hear him speak. The person can draw an inductive inference that (it is probable or likely) the next time he teaches on rhetoric, he will draw large crowds. The conclusion is based on the belief that the future resembles the past, and these past experiences may be valuable to the person who may want to arrive early the next time to be in front to hear the great orator speak. Anything of course can interrupt the certainty of this inductive pattern of Aristotle drawing large crowds, such as, one may on the same day, and at the same time, prefer to hear Plato speak. Or even a person who drives a certain route to work every day, and observes each time they drive this particular way they encoutner a delay in traffic. Is this not valuable induction for the person who may choose to take another route or to leave early to be punctual for work? This is still valuable information albeit not scientific.

Obviously, Aristotle's induction goes beyond personal experience and practical matters, as Joseph A. Novak states: "An examination of multiple passages in Aristotle should make it clear that the terminus of the process of induction is not simply the grasp of a simple essence whose multiple instances have provided an experiential base for its cognitive apprehension in a simple intuition."[9] History has demonstrated that many discoveries are ingrained in induction. William Jevons states:

> We learn empirically that a certain strong yellow color at sunset, or an unusual clearness in the air, portends rain; that a quick pulse fever; that horned animals ruminates;

8. Groarke, "Jumping the Gaps," 459.
9. Novak, "Socrates and Induction," 202.

Introduction to Aristotle

that quinine affects beneficially the nervous system and the health of the body generally; that strychnine has a terrible effect of the opposite nature; all these are known to be repeated observation, but we can give no other reason for their being true, that is, we cannot bring them into harmony with any other scientific facts; nor could we at all have deduced them or anticipated them on the grounds of previous knowledge.[10]

These inductive observations, and the knowledge that are grounded in them, all the necessary medical information does not have to be available to make these inductive judgments, this does not preclude that further investigation of the causes of things are not warranted, and more development in the medical profession are not compulsory. What if, we wait until all inductions are completely enumerated to decide what a thing is, we would certainly fall short of the contributions of induction: practically, spiritually, medically, and scientifically. Another point that needs to be made about induction, is that induction seeks more than inference and generalities, it seeks to discover the nature of something. A child will quickly learn that touching a hot iron burns (perhaps after one or two encounters), and will soon realize every time and everywhere he or she touches a hot iron it will burn.[11] We also know that fire generates heat, but induction wants to know and explain why fire is hot and why it draws heat. Let us put it this way: "Induction is not so much about determining how many times fire is associated with heat; it more about understanding what fire is and why it produces heat."[12]

---

10. Thilly, *Process of Inductive Inference*, 33.

11. The question remains—and it is an important one—from where does this leap or gap come? How do we move from sense perception and experience to concepts? The stimulus that undergirds this inductive leap or creativity derive from nous or possibly some inspirational element that is beyond self that grants insight into the object or subject. We do not jump from a particular to another particular experience of the same kind mindlessly, we cross over these horizons by nous that mental capacity that allows us to grasp things. That bridges the gap.

12. Groarke, *Aristotelian Account of Induction*, 148–49.

Induction and Example

To the last point. In the pecking order of reasoning, "induction comes first in the process of knowledge formation; deduction comes second."[13] To use induction to explain deduction is to "put the cart before the horse."[14] Aristotle explains, "First principles are more knowable than demonstrations, and all scientific knowledge involves reason. It follows that there can be no scientific knowledge of the first principles; and since nothing can be more infallible than scientific knowledge except intuition, it must be intuition that apprehends the first principles."[15] So if there is an attack on the process of induction there is ultimately an attack on deductive reasoning, and if the inductive conclusion is false surely the deduction is false also.[16]

If one holds to the belief that the origin of humanity started with the "Adam" in Genesis 1–2, the first man did not deduce the reality of God based on any deductive claims, this human first experienced God inductively (i.e., through revelation or God's personal presence) before any notion of deducing God's existence. Before there was a concept or theology of sin there was first Adam's experience of God without sin. The initial inductive sin experience led to the universal concept, and then we deduce the concept. Without the experience there is no concept. If deductive arguments attempts to demonstrate God's existence, it is induction that we experience God's existence.

Summary

Induction requires a leap in the reasoning process, in which the conclusion produces more evidence than stated in the premises, but this does not negate the credibility of inductive reasoning, nor does this denote the leap is baseless or prone to hypotheticals. Moreover, the mind or perhaps a spiritual enlightenment bridges

---

13. Groarke, "Jumping the Gaps," 513.
14. Groarke, "Jumping the Gaps," 513.
15. Aristotle, *An. post.* 2.19.
16. Groarke, *Aristotelian Account of Induction*, 162.

the gap between one particular and another particular experience. One does not have to examine an object or subject for eternity to make a genuine inductive claim, but only see that a relationship exists between several cases of the same kind.

2

Aristotle's Example
(Gk. Paradeigma)

Scholars have not sufficiently considered Aristotle's rhetorical example, and this lack of devotion is probably due to both their and Aristotle's greater emphasis on deductive arguments. Even though example is tailored more so for the nontechnical audience, and the reasoning process is not as high-profile as deductive reasoning, this disproportion is not because example lacks credibility or persuasive power; Aristotle explains example produces conviction just as the enthymeme.[1] Nor should we conjure up the notion that the orator lack argumentative skills by using the example instead of deductive arguments (several factors contribute to which form of reasoning the orator uses, namely, the audience, the location, the type of speech, and the rhetorical aim). The example still requires artistic imagination and logical formation. This process also requires judicious research skills to discover applicable historical or present examples constructed for the argumentative situation. This must be done to effectively appeal to and persuade the target audience.

---

1. Aristotle, *An. post.* 1.1. For information on English translations referenced throughout this book, see bibliography.

Aristotle's Example

The Distinction between Aristotle's Induction and Example

The distinctive nature of induction and example do not share the same method because they arrive at different conclusions.² The main difference is that "induction stops after the generalization is formed, whereas example continues on to apply this generalization to another particular instance, and, second, induction examines all of the particulars while example does not."³ Induction is the source material for the paradeigma and so induction is its cornerstone.

Schollmeier points out that the best way to describe the difference between the two methodologies is that induction proper is a logical technique, and the example is a rhetorical technique.⁴ Let us follow this proposition. The logical technique, as Aristotle explains:

> Induction, or inductive reasoning, consists in establishing a relation between one extreme term and the middle term by means of the other extreme; e.g., if B is the middle term of A and C, in proving by means of C that A applies to B; for this is how we effect inductions. E.g., let A stand for "long-lived," B for "that which has no bile" and C for the long-lived individuals such as man and horse and mule. Then A applies to the whole of C [for every bileless animal is long lived]. But B, "not having bile," also applies to all C.⁵

Let us restate the illustration: we have one extreme term (A) "long-lived" joining another extreme term (C) namely, "man and horse and mule." Now "instead of having a middle term joining the two extremes, we have a subject term that allows us to join the middle to

---

2. Aristotle asserts that example "differs from induction in that the later, as we saw, shows from an examination of all the individual cases that the <major> extreme applies to the middle, and does not connect the conclusion with the <minor> extreme; whereas the example does connect it and does not use all the individual cases for its proof." Aristotle, *An. pr.* 2.24.

3. Benoit, "Aristotle's Example," 188.

4. Schollmeier, "Problem of Example," 233.

5. Aristotle, *An. pr.* 2.23.

Induction and Example

the predicate term."⁶ Bileless animals are long-lived. We can explain the induction further, "All men, horses, mules, etc., are long-lived; all men, horses, mules, etc., are bileless; therefore, all bileless animals are long-lived."⁷ Members of this class, namely, men, horses, mules, possess certain properties such as being bileless.

To illustrate the rhetorical technique, Aristotle explains example in *Prior Analytics*:

> Then if we require to prove that war against Thebes is bad, we must be satisfied that war against neighbors is bad. Evidence of this can be drawn from similar examples, e.g., that war by Thebes against Phocis is bad. Then since war against neighbors is bad, and war against Thebes is against neighbors, it is evident that war against Thebes is bad. Now it is evident that B applies to C and D (for they are both examples of making war on neighbors), and A to D (since the war against Phocis did Thebes no good); but that A applies to B will be proved by means of D.⁸

In this multifaceted example, Aristotle's argument by example is explained in letters. He informs the readers on how to structure the rhetorical argument, and how to prove that going to war against Thebes is a bad idea, and therefore going to war with one's neighbor is a bad idea. Groarke explains that Aristotle "proposes a two stage strategy" for accomplishing this:

> We must first establish the general principle "that war against neighbors is ruinous." We can do this by arguing that Thebes waging war against Phocis was ruinous and that Thebes making war against Phocis was war against neighbors, so that all war against neighbors is ruinous. . . . But once we have established that all war against

---

6. Groarke, *Aristotelian Account of Induction*, 125.

7. Groarke, *Aristotelian Account of Induction*, 125. He also explains, "In deduction, the middle term joins the two extremes; in induction, one extreme, the subject term, acts as the middle term, joining the true middle with the other extreme" (126).

8. Aristotle, *An. pr.* 2.24. Aristotle states beforehand that let A be "bad," B "to make war on neighbors," C "Athens against Thebes," and D "Thebes against Phocis."

neighbors is ruinous, we can deduce that Athens going to war against Thebes would be ruinous. This is, we can make the following deduction. "War against neighbors is ruinous; a war by Athens against Thebes would be war against a neighbor; so a war between Athens and Thebes would be ruinous."[9]

The generalization that the example forms is depicted and applied to the present case and a conclusion is drawn.[10] In order for the example to have efficacy, the audience must participate in understanding the significance of the example that war against neighbors is bad.

To explain further the rhetorical technique, in King Agrippa's great speech to the Jews, which deals with matters that are both contingent and rhetorical. He advises the Jews not to revolt against Roman authorities because Rome had historically defeated many countries that rose up against it to fight for their liberties. To support his argument, King Agrippa cites historical examples, the fall of powerful nations, such as the Athenians and the Macedonians.[11] We can restate the argument in syllogistic form: the powerful countries, namely, the Athenians and the Macedonians, lost their battles with Rome; Jews are less powerful than the Athenians and the Macedonians; therefore Jews would lose a battle with Rome. We deduce that the Athenians' and Macedonians' desire to revolt against Rome was detrimental and that their attempt to fight for their liberties were attempts to revolt, and so the Jews' attempt to fight for their liberties is an attempt to revolt and will be detrimental.

Aristotle's Entechnic Proofs

Aristotle informs us that "there are two kinds of examples; namely, one which consists in relating things that have happened before, and

---

9. Groarke, *Aristotelian Account of Induction*, 218–19.
10. Hauser, "The Example in Aristotle's Rhetoric," 86.
11. Josephus, *Complete Works*, 486–90.

Induction and Example

another in inventing them oneself."[12] The first *entechnic* (artistic) proof, the historical example, is measured as a factual event that occurred in time and space. Although the example is lodged in history, we must not gloss over that a certain level of ingenuity still remains because the proof is contextually shaped for the current audience.

The other two artistic proofs are the analogy (parable) and the fable; as with the historical paradeigma, they too are rhetorical and rely on similarities. Groarke adds, that "arguments by analogy are a weaker type of inductive inference employed to secure opinion, instead of scientific fact. They produce general conclusions admitting of exceptions. They yield a fallible grasp of some contingent or accidental likeness."[13] The analogy is particularly useful for comparing parallel cases and the logical movement is from particular to particular. The third classification of the example is the fable. The fable can be drawn from various things such as speaking animals or inanimate objects. Aristotle explains:

> Fables are suitable for public speaking, and they have this advantage that, while it is difficult to find similar things that have really happened in the past, it is easier to invent fables; for they must be invented, like comparisons, if a man is capable of seizing the analogy; and this is easy if one studies philosophy. Thus, while the lessons conveyed by fables are easier to provide, those derived from facts are more useful for deliberative oratory, because as a rule the future resembles the past.[14]

Eugene Garver asserts that "telling a fable or referring to an invented parable does not destroy credibility, as a farfetched argument does."[15] The fable substantiates history and thus practical reality, which Garver argues emphasizes credibility.

---

12. Aristotle, *Rhet.* 2:20.
13. Groarke, *Aristotelian Account of Induction*, 215.
14. Aristotle, *Rhet.* 2.20.
15. Garver, *Aristotle's Rhetoric*, 158.

Aristotle's Historical Example

Let us delve into the specifics of Aristotle's historical example. First and foremost, his examples are not an anthology of narrations of noble events and people of the past nor randomly chosen texts, but rather selective proofs. Aristotle affords us an archetypal historical example:

> It would be an instance of the historical kind of example, if one were to say that it is necessary to make preparations against the great King and not to allow him to subdue Egypt; for Darius did not crossover to Greece until he had obtained possession of Egypt; but as soon as he had done so, he did. Again, Xerxes did not attack us until he had obtained possession of that country, but when he had, he crossed over; consequently, if the present Great King shall do the same, he will cross over, wherefore it must not be allowed.[16]

Aristotle employs two (historical) examples of conquering kings, Darius and Xerxes, that forms the one example text.[17] The first example is of no greater force or authoritative than the second one. The second example of Xerxes nevertheless reinforces the pattern of the first example of Darius the king of Persia. The two Aristotelian paradeigmata are rhetorical, and meant to persuade the contemporary audience to reject a particular position and behavior in the future. Both examples are applicable because they fall within the same class and intended purpose of the Great King.

The audience share insight with the orator, in understanding the behavior of the leaders, who they are and what they inspire to do.[18] That Darius and Xerxes plan of action were to cross over into Greece after conquering Egypt.[19] If the Great King is allowed to cross over he will conquer the territory as the other leaders, this will

---

16. Aristotle, *Rhet.* 2.20.3.
17. Novak, "Socrates and Induction," 216.
18. Ryan, *Aristotle's Theory of Rhetorical Argumentation*, 122.
19. Lyons, *Exemplum*, 25.

Induction and Example

be to their disadvantage. The decision must be drawn therefore by the Greeks that the Great King must not be allowed to do so.

John D. Lyons observes that "the example of the Great King, no attempt is made to compare the whole of the life of different kings. Instead a single sequence of acts is selected from the biographies of the various kings to be set forth in an example cluster."[20] Nonessential elements of their biographical history were left out, and to include them would compromise the integrity and conciseness of the example. Moreover, Aristotle's example is not restricted to Greece, he explores examples that extend to the territory of Persia. The deliberative orator must not only examine the results of his own state, but also those carried on by others because Aristotle believes that "similar results naturally arise from similar causes."[21]

Lyons also points out that "the example of the Great King does not itself contain the word example or any synonym thereof."[22] This missing linguistic indicator is however replaced by the preposition "for." After the presumed tactics of the present Great King, the preposition "for" introduces the historical example of Darius and Xerxes. The analogy is therefore made between the past and present, but the example also requires a future response. All three tenses describe the continuous thread of the example, and the individuals who encompass the example. The past tense action of Darius and Xerxes, the present action of the Great King, and the future action by the Greeks still remain unknown.

In another historical illustration, Aristotle states:

> To prove that Dionysius is aiming at a tyranny, because he asks for a bodyguard, one might say that Pisistratus before him and Theagenes of Megara did the same, and when they obtained what they asked for made themselves tyrants. All the other tyrants known may serve as an example of Dionysius, whose reason, however, for asking for a bodyguard we do not yet know. All these examples

---

20. Lyons, *Exemplum*, 31.
21. Aristotle, *Rhet.* 1.4.9.
22. Lyons, *Exemplum*, 26.

Aristotle's Example

are contained under the same universal proposition, that one who is aiming at a tyranny asks for a bodyguard.[23]

Aristotle wishes to prove the ambitions of Dionysius who asks for a bodyguard. In order to expose his intentions, he ushers in the example of Pisistratus and Theagenes. Unless the rhetor is highly skilled in developing a single historical example, and the example is considered the standard of events or behaviors of which standards are measured, it would be difficult to persuade anyone based on a single case because a pattern of events or behaviors are not yet established. Nevertheless, like the previous example of Darius and Xerxes, the example of Pisistratus and Theagenes are equally authoritative.

The auditors can readily identify with the ethos of these leaders in which their goals are fully disclosed. Aristotle does not explicitly indicate the function of their ethos that is within the historical example, yet these leaders' ethos undeniably contribute in understanding the example.[24] Thus "one argues from the known intentions of Pisistratus and Theagenes (and possibly others known to the listeners) to the hitherto unknown intentions of Dionysius. . . . The individuals are in the same class to a lesser known one."[25] The known cases of Pisistratus and Theagenes serve the present case of Dionysius, although his actions still remain unknown.

An important point should be made here, although similar results might arise from similar causes, there is no guarantee this is true in each and every case. Groarke explains, "The argument is intended to be persuasive or plausible rather than rigorous. Waging war on one's neighbors is not necessarily ruinous. Nor does it necessarily follow that someone who asks for a bodyguard *must* be scheming to make himself a despot."[26] Asking for a bodyguard has more than one purpose besides making oneself a despot.

---

23. Aristotle, *Rhet.* 1.2.19.
24. Brinton, "Cicero's Use of Historical Examples," 175–77.
25. Ryan, *Aristotle's Theory of Rhetorical Argumentation*, 118.
26. Groarke, *Aristotelian Account of Induction*, 219.

Induction and Example

Aristotle's Example: Part to Whole to Part

We have stated there is a leap in the inductive process, and therefore according to philosophers, we have a problem with induction. We also have a problem with the movement of the example that philosophers and scholars have to tackle. In Aristotle's explanation of the example, he asserts the relationship of the example to the proposition "is neither the relation of part to whole, nor of one whole to another whole, but of part to part, of like to like, when both come under the same genus."[27] At first blush, this statement appears straightforward and simplistic in form, but scholars differ as to the exact meaning of the phrase. Does Aristotle mean "part to part, or like to like," to be interpreted at face value that is, from one particular to another particular without a generalization or universal or are we to infer it as an unmediated generalization, an abbreviation for a concealed universal? Benoit believes:

> When Aristotle characterizes example as movement from "part to part" it is clear that this is shorthand for "part to whole to part" and that just as rhetors often leave the whole implicit, so too does Aristotle in this description. The rhetor assumes the whole during invention, the generalization connects the two parts, the two parts belong to the same genus, and the examples are part of the same universal.[28]

Hauser contends, however, that Aristotle's depiction of "part-to-part" should be taken literally and that "this is the way in which [Aristotle] believed the argument from example literally was formed and literally functioned as a reasoning process for listeners."[29] There are definite reasons why one would subscribe to "part to part" as a straight parallel between similar cases, as typically assumed that a direct comparison is in view, and not a universal. Groarke points out that in Aristotle's work:

---

27. Aristotle, *Rhet.* 1.2.19.
28. Benoit, "On Aristotle's Example," 264.
29. Hauser, "Aristotle's Example Revisited," 172.

Aristotle's Example

The movement is always from a particular up to a general class and then back down to another particular.... Logically construed, two particular inference from analogy must move from the particular up to the universal and back down to another particular. We secure a properly logical conclusion, not from the bare fact that particular cases resemble one another but from the inclusion of each case in the larger group.[30]

The point is that the example is not restricted to these particular cases but other similar cases. Reguero concludes that "παραδειγμα, understood as a process of inference, implies a double argument, since it supposes a first inductive part, in which from concrete cases (illustrantia) a universal proposition established as a major premise until reaching the demonstration of the new concrete case (illustrandum)."[31] I concur that Aristotle's historical examples functions rhetorically in the sense that the whole may be implicit or explicit. He used Pisistratus and Theagenes analogically who both were considered tyrants because they ask for bodyguards this generates the universal principle. Aristotle does not say that applies only to this particular case, but rather all known cases or tyrants who ask for a bodyguard.[32] In both historical examples listed above, Aristotle employs two examples to reinforce his proposition, but also to form a generalization or universal.

Deliberative Examples in Oratorical Speeches

The kind of speech delivered by an orator corresponds with the purpose of the oration, and since a deliberative speech focuses on future decisions, it primarily uses examples to persuade or dissuade a particular audience that a certain course of action is to their advantage and best interest.[33] Aristotle points out:

30. Groarke, *Aristotelian Account of Induction*, 219–20.
31. Reguero, "Example and Similarity," 242.
32. Aristotle, *Rhet.* 1.2.19.
33. Aristotle, *Rhet.* 1.9.40.

Induction and Example

> The aim before the deliberative orator is that which is expedient, and men deliberate, not about the end, but about the means to the end, which are the things which are expedient in regard to our actions; and since, further, the expedient is good, we must first grasp the elementary notions of good and expedient in general.[34]

In Aristotle's account of deliberative oratory the focus is not the end result, but rather it is advising what is expedient and is trying to convince the audience the best possible way to achieve those means to an end. It is insufficient for a deliberative orator to proclaim victory is ours if we believe, he must demonstrate the best course of action to achieve those ends or victory. Speaking before the Jews, King Agrippa understood the expedient, presenting alternatives: choose life by not revolting or choose death in pursuance of an unwinnable battle. Agrippa did not pull up their past to convince them not to revolt, he tried to persuade them how they should proceed in the future. Since the Jews heeded his plea, hundreds or even thousands of Jews were saved.

A deliberative orator must also possess rhetorical skills and facilitate the various forms of argumentation and their opposites to effectively argue. The orator must be acquainted with the peculiars of the audience, weighing different options, and determining what is in their best interest in the future. Thus there is more to employing examples than simply reaching back in history and discovering similar characteristics, but how to constitute the example for the present audience. Although the expedient is a corollary of a paradeigma, other elements of arguments by example are a derivative of this specie. Aristotle explains, things "such as justice and injustice, honor and disgrace, are included as accessory in reference to this."[35] For instance, epideictic rhetoric typically occurs in the public domain in the present. It emphasizes ceremonial oration; praise and blame or virtue and vice. A deliberative orator may use the virtue of a (courageous) person in the present to persuade his audience to emulate the same type of courageousness in the future.

34. Aristotle, *Rhet.* 1.6.1.
35. Aristotle, *Rhet* 1.3.5.

Aristotle's Example

Comprehension and Persuasiveness of Examples

First and foremost, the simplistic nature of example does not diminish the persuasive power of example, as King Agrippa's speech demonstrates. He was able to slow down the tension by painting a clearer picture of the end result based on past examples. Agrippa's rhetoric succeeded because the examples were built on truth, and gives evidence behind that truth not built on empty rhetoric. The Jews could not rebuff the end results of past nations that were mightier than them militarily, in wealth, bountiful in ships, numerous in men and allies. The logic behind Agrippa's speech, if the Jews are unequal to any of those nations in all such categories, how do they believe they will come out victorious? Aristotle reminds us if an orator's speech is based on truth it is easier to persuade than if the speech was built on falsehood.[36] Even the Dalmatians who frequently insurrected in hopes of securing their liberties (despite their continuous efforts to revolt) still ended up subsuming to Roman rule.

It is apparent King Agrippa understood the attitude and beliefs of his Jewish audience, and the history of warfare of other nations which was essential to his argument. He prepared his speech that was not in violation of their Judaic conscious, nor did he attempt to violate their core values. One of the essential tenets of example being successful in persuading an audience, it must be reasonable. Eugene Ryan explains the example must "fall under the same genus [which] is a necessary condition for the argument's being reasonable."[37] If the examples were outside the Jews understanding and seeing their situation in it, the likelihood of the examples been convincing would be rather bleak.[38] If an orator is unable to persuade (besides lacking rhetorical skill) his audience, perhaps he was inept in the collection of proofs or imprecise in accessing the audience state of affairs correctly.

36. Aristotle, *Rhet.* 1.1.12–14.

37. Ryan also explains that "Aristotle criticized Plato for trying to construct an argument about human society using as paradigms wild beasts, and labeled the attempt absurd or unreasonable." Ryan, *Aristotle's Theory of Rhetorical Argumentation*, 134.

38. Ryan, *Aristotle's Theory of Rhetorical Argumentation*, 134.

Induction and Example

Aristotle's examples listed above are simplistic in nature and do not require considerable intellectual inquiry to determine the intentions of particular individuals. It is relatively clear the audience could deduce that if the Great King is allowed to cross over similarly to Darius and Xerxes, it will be to their disadvantage and detriment.[39]

Summary

Aristotle points out the enthymeme and the example are the only way to produce conviction, and although he devotes great energy in explaining the enthymeme, he does not consider the example least effective in arguing one's case. He employs several kinds of example, the historical example, the analogy, and the fable, all of which are used to support propositions in the present. And unlike the analogy and fable, which usually moves from one particular to another particular, the historical example, however, contains a universal proposition. Since the primary objective of example is to persuade an audience that a certain course of action is in their best interest, the example is better suited for deliberative rhetoric because every so often the future resembles the past. Another reason an orator employs an example is that they are easier to grasps than deductive arguments.

---

39. In the *Topics*, Aristotle states, "For clearness, examples and illustrations should be adduced, the examples being to the point and drawn from things which are familiar to us, of the kind which Homer uses and not of the kind that Choerilus employs; for thus the proposition would be rendered clearer." Aristotle, *Top.* 8.1.

3

Induction

Observation and Experience

INDUCTION ENTAILS MAKING AN inference from one particular experience to another of the same kind, in which one sees that a similarity exist; the human mind has the capacity to grasp patterns, natures, causes, logical relationships, etc. A person may have a certain kind of experience, and this same kind of experience is repeated again, and again, the person may infer that these experiences are somehow related, so the next time he or she encounters the same type of experience, it is possible the experience will happen again in the future. A person who believes in Christ, let us call her Bernice, believes that God in Christ has delivered her from a particular affliction in the past, and another particular affliction, these two deliverances and experiences become stored memory facts. If she encounters another affliction that requires a healing, she depends on these past memory facts and (making the noetic and spiritual connection between her past and present experience) takes comfort in knowing that God has delivered her before and God is able to deliver again.[1] To be sure, Bernice is thinking

---

1. It is important to note that although she acknowledges God as a healer, this does not guarantee that any future afflictions she encounters will yield the same results.

Induction and Example

inductively rather than deductively in making her conclusions.[2] Her inductive experiences now turn into personal examples of God as a healer, and becomes the argumentative source for her deductive claims; thus her induction precedes her deduction. She concludes deductively: God is a healer, God has healed me, and therefore God is a healer. Her personal knowledge of God as a healer, will ultimately become the evangelistic material to testify that God is a real presence in her life, and to invite others to join the community of faith.

As we take a closer look into the peculiarities of NT induction (observation and experience), biblical writers often explicate how particular events disclose the nature of their reality, and the reality of others. Subsequently, those who are invested and progress in the induction often make substantial knowledge claims forming generalization and/or universal conclusions. Some inductions, however, lead to valid conclusions, and other inductions reveal flawed inductive reasoning or conclusions. To be sure, the writers do not give a scientific explanation but a spiritual one of these personal, or community experiences, they all take on the form of inductive reasoning, which explain how they reached their inductive conclusion.

Observation

The notion of observation is the capacity to perceive objects as they exist in time and space; when we observe a particular object or subject, we often depending on the perceptual engagement discriminate not all the properties they possess, but only certain characteristics at a given point in time. These observations makes an impression on our cognition, emotions, and character. This enables us to accrue

---

2. A follower of Christ may not have complete trust in God at the beginning of his or her religious experience, but the first experience is nevertheless the cornerstone in the trusting and believing process. For instance, Paul's experience "did not come in its fullness all at once . . . but, as Paul saw it, it was all implicit in the Damascus-road revelation." Bruce, *Paul*, 80.

Induction

knowledge of what we observe, and interpret what we observe, and ultimately draw conclusions about what we observe.³

Interpreting Biblical Observation

As we embark on examining NT observations, we observe that the identity and ministry of Jesus were observed (miracles, healings, signs and wonders, etc.) and confirmed firsthand by more than a few, but many eye witnesses bear testimony to his ministry, even those outside the faith testified to his character and events. The author of 1 John asserts that the identity of Jesus came (not exclusively) through sense perception, he states "that which was from the beginning, which we have heard, which we have seen with our eyes, which we have looked at and our hands have touched—this we proclaim concerning the Word of life" (1:1). He points out three particular sensory qualities: sight, hearing, and touch, each sensory organ was the starting point that revealed knowledge to the reality of Jesus' identity and character. In addition, the deeds performed by both Peter and Paul were also observed and legitimized by numerous eyewitnesses in the early church, and those outside the church.

In Luke 7:19, John the Baptist sent two disciples to ask about the identity of Jesus, stating, "Are you the one who is to come, or should we expect someone else?" In 7:22, Jesus responds, "Go back and report to John what you have seen and heard: The blind receive sight, the lame walk, those who have leprosy are cleansed, the deaf hear, the dead are raised." The eyewitness testimony of these particular events reveal knowledge of Jesus' true identity and ministry. He did not attempt to explicate his messiahship through self-promotion or deductive arguments, instead he uses the observation from others to substantiate his statement, and even to postulate a universal claim for his identity:

1. The induction is "look at the evidence" and draw an inference from what you see and hear that will tell you who he

---

3. See appendix on sense perception and observation.

Induction and Example

is. He heals the blind man with his spit, heals the centurion's daughter, and raises Lazarus from the dead.

2. The greater number of particular or individual instances where Jesus performed miracles strengthens the universal claim of his identity. The miracles of Jesus fit into a universal category such as "healing the sick" or "raising the dead."

3. Therefore, a universal conclusion can be drawn—Jesus must be the Messiah.

Jesus simply instructs them to go back and tell John what you have observed, and he will draw his conclusion from the evidence.

In Aristotle's logic, this might look like the following arguments: Anyone who does the miracles foretold in scripture is the Messiah. (There is only one Messiah but this is still a universal claim. It says that anyone who would do this is the Messiah.) Jesus works the miracles foretold in scripture. Therefore Jesus is the Messiah. So this is deductive proof—or demonstration—that Jesus is the Messiah.

In Matt 27:45–54, the Roman centurion who guards Jesus' tomb observes with other spectators and recognizes the phenomenal nature of the events, which happens through a cluster of progressive observational experiences: "the darkness, the earthquake, and the cry of dereliction convinced the solders that this was no ordinary execution."[4] These events had such a profound effect on the centurion and those with him, they subsequently concluded these omens must be a testimony to heaven's wrath.[5] We are reminded these sequential events (that took place within a span of three hours) were not based on any revelatory experience or because the soldiers were innately aware of Jesus' identity, rather these soldiers secured their induction through sensory perception. Hearing and sight were the starting point that allowed them to understand his identity. Although this was an emotional response to the events, it was also an exercise of progressive induction, which produced the conclusion; that Jesus was the son of God Matt 27:54.

4. Carson, *Matthew*, 583.
5. Carson, *Matthew*, 583.

Induction

In Matt 17:4, Peter wishes to immortalize the event at the Mount of Transfiguration through the conduits of induction. This was not a common inductive experience but an extraordinary one that should have catapulted him to a greater understanding of Jesus' identity and mission. This experience was to prepare Peter and the other two disciples of what was to come. In these passages, Peter erroneously moves to a hasty generalization (as he seldom did) without truly comprehending and evaluating the true nature of the event, stating, "Lord, it is good for us to be here. If you wish, I will put up three shelters—one for you, one for Moses and one for Elijah." It is not that Peter's sensible perception is deceived or he failed to observe the particular event in time and space, rather he overly spiritualized and was caught up in the emotion of the experience, thus drawing a false conclusion.[6] He assumes that the appearance of all three men proposes an equal inductive relationship that exist, and therefore a tabernacle should be built; one for Moses, one for Elijah, and one for Jesus. If all three men's missions were similar in divine purpose and scope, Peter's inductive insight on building three tabernacles would have been acceptable and legitimate. The primary reason Peter's inductive reasoning failed, however, was because Jesus' mission and purpose was superior to Moses and Elijah's. His ministry was validated when a voice out of the cloud told Peter, James and John that it is Jesus who they must listen to. We must bear in mind that although Peter's induction failed the test, the induction did reveal what is true and what is not.

To the last observation. Induction does not begin with argumentation but rather insight into the phenomenon. This type of "reasoning begins in the mental activity of induction, understood not as an argument form, but as a mental realization triggered by sense perception.... This is where thought begins, with induction understood as an intuitive cognitive capacity."[7] It is the ability to internalize the first stages of observation and see that a relationship exist, even before the need to argue deductively.

---

6. See appendix on sense perception.
7. Groarke, *Aristotelian Account of Induction*, 9.

Induction and Example

In Matt 6:25–34, Jesus had the ability to observe nature and see a pattern of existence about particular species. He first observes triggered by sense perception (not through any argumentative form) the natural tendency of fowl life, and then through a flash of insight ("aha moment") gained recognition into the activity of this particular specie.[8] As the word ἐμβλέψατε, or "look," suggests, Jesus observed instantly or possibly through previous multiple inductive observations of the actions of the "fowls of the air," and recognized—this is what they do (Matt 6:26). In another instance, Jesus asks his disciples to cogitate the lilies of the field and recognize their natural disposition; he identified, "they do not labor or spin" (Matt 6:28).

In both observations, Jesus observed nature to address a human experience and predicament. He recognizes that the "fowls of the air" and the "lilies of the field" have a natural dependency on God's providence. After the inductive process of birds and lilies are formed, Jesus takes the observed actions of "fowls" and "lilies" that generates the example, and then rhetorically applies the generalization to the particular case of the disciple's lack of trust for things in this life (6:27–32). The rhetorical significance is the comparison moves from the lesser "fowls of the air" and "lilies of the field," to the greater "disciples" or "humanity," οὐχ ὑμεῖς μᾶλλον διαφέρετε αὐτῶν; or "Are you not much more valuable than they" (v. 26)? Hagner states, "If disciples are worth more than birds, then they may be assured of God's providential care for their needs just as certainly as the birds depend on God for theirs."[9] The inductive observations Jesus employs are meant for the first-century disciple, but also for every disciple in every generation who lacks trust in God's providential care.

---

8. I use Louis Groarke's term "recognition."
9. Hagner, *Matthew 1–13*, 164.

Induction

Experience

A considerable amount of NT texts were born and transcribed out of experience, the authors may have been inspired to write not separate from their experience, but by means of their experience. If we remove the experiences the ancients had with Christ (in the gospels), what remains (besides the death, burial, resurrection and ascension) is nothing more than meaningless pages. The gospels writers disclose not mundane experiences per se, rather relevant, pivotal and extraordinary experiences that furnish knowledge of the reality of Christ, and his mission. Just as the revelation of God came to humanity through experience,[10] the revelation of Christ likewise came to the citizens of the first century through experience. Many theologies and ideologies were surely canonized based on the apostles, and the early church experiences.[11]

Even though Apostle Paul did not have the distinction to walk with Jesus during his earthly ministry, it did nothing to diminish his profound experience with him. He became a chosen vessel and beacon light for him, he left on record his initial encounter with Christ and subsequent experiences whether through revelations, visions or dreams or some other form of communication, these experiences shaped who he was, and what he was to become in the history of the church. Other biblical writers describe individual accounts of their experiences of God in Christ; see in particular Acts and Revelation.

---

10. Lane, *Experience of God*, 53.

11. Salvation history did not occur apart from the human experience, but by means of that experience. In the OT, the God of Israel was not isolated from the children of Israel's wilderness experience, but rather was in the midst of their experience. Moreover, God worked through Joseph's experience with Pharaoh in Genesis, and Joshua when the walls of Jericho tumbled. Even the psalmist states in 37:25, "I was young and now I am old, yet I have never seen the righteous forsaken or their children begging bread." The writer contends he never witness in his lifetime through personal observation that God was unable to provide.

Induction and Example

The Experience of the Theologian and the Lay Person

There is a distinction between a lay person who has experienced God and a theologian or scholar who has studied God and knows various systematics and attributes of God. Those who experience God inductively or should I say, those who have an interconnection with God may know just as much about God as do those who have studied God academically, but have not experienced God on a personally level. Angelo Scola makes the point:

> In the first place, we have to remember that Christian experience is ontologically prior to theology. It is theology's proper horizon, whereas the reverse is not the case. Theology, understood as systematic and critical investigation, is in itself incapable of producing Christian experience by its own resources. What is more, theology is born of Christian experience and must ceaselessly refer to the horizon that this experience sets for it. Given this premise, there are good grounds for saying that every crisis of theology—provided that the requirements of its object and the rigor of its method have been ensured—has its ultimate explanation in a crisis of Christian experience.[12]

Even those who are skilled in dogma are reliant on the Christian experience (through biblical passages) to grasp and comprehend the nature of God that is, as much as a finite being can understand the nature of the infinite being.[13] In view of this, the lay person or parishioner who is not trained in theology perhaps may not have the erudition to elucidate God's providential care on a scholarly level with specialization, but this inability does not prevent him or her from explaining the providence of God heuristically. Even if the lay person or parishioner are not scholastic or proficient theologically, they are still able to do theology because their experience of God teaches them to do theology. There is an adage that those who experience God, know God best.

12. Scola, *Christian Experience and Theology*, 1–3.
13. Scola, *Christian Experience and Theology*, 1–3.

Induction

Interpreting Biblical Experience

In Acts, the vision of Cornelius (10:1–8) and Peter's vision (10:9–16) describe how both visionary experiences were in concert with the overall purpose of God, and how God uses Peter as an instrument for religious and social change. These events transforms Peter's social reality, theology, and evangelistic activities. As the narrative explains, Peter's visionary experience about eating unclean animals or things impure was not self-interpretive because he was oblivious to the direct meaning (10:17, 19), neither did Cornelius know the exact implication of his vision, he was only told his prayers were heard, and was instructed to search out Peter who held the keys to the interpretation of the vision. Every so often the meaning and interpretation behind an experience is not presently disclosed, the implication of it often come to light in stages or later in a person's life.[14]

In this regard, Peter's spiritual awareness, and the significance behind his vision, were grasped through nous (the mind) and (the Spirit instructions) secured only in the context of Cornelius's vision, and the events that took place afterward. Peter could now comprehend the true meaning behind the symbolism of God's creatures and that all were declared clean by God, and therefore Cornelius is likewise declared clean.[15] The inductive leap moved from Cornelius's particular case to Peter's particular case to a universal conclusion (both visions were of the same class of accepting Gentiles by God). He can say unequivocally, "I now realize [through personal experience in which I can affirm for myself] how true it is that God does not show favoritism."[16] If God is not a respecter of person and does not discriminate between Jew and Gentile surely Peter cannot be a respecter of person. It was Peter's

---

14. Lane, *Experience of God*, 22–23.

15. Polhill, *Acts*, 258.

16. Although his transformed theological convictions had ramifications for the inclusion of Gentiles here, his position radically changed in Antioch (Gal 2:11–14).

Induction and Example

encounter and experience with God that brought to light his theology of God.

Even though Peter discovers a truth about God's character that was previously outside his spiritual awareness, we must not overlook God had to first remove the initial opposition of partiality the esteem apostle exhibited about the significance of his vision, otherwise Peter would have upheld the notion of fraternizing with Gentiles (10:28). This reminds us that people who encounter a fresh religious experience are never truly free from their belief system, nor do they begin from a tabula rasa, but often use their past traditions and religiosities to interpret their present experience.[17] This new inductive insight would allow Peter to break down the barriers of distinction and eat, and associate with Cornelius, and his household unabated without any religious and social restrictions (10:9–48).

I would add the momentous work of God traveled, but the same spiritual work accepted in Caesarea was challenged by some Jews in the Jerusalem church, who did not embrace Peter eating with Gentiles (10:24—11:18). Like Peter demonstrated, strict adherers of religiosity are unwilling to relinquish long standing traditions, nor are they willing to welcome change when it goes against their theology and ideologies. Peter will nevertheless quell such criticism by recounting both visionary experiences that explained God was behind the visions, and the orchestrator of ethnic, social, and religious change. The proof and the end result that Peter provides affirm that during his message about Jesus Christ, the Spirit fell on Gentiles as the Spirit fell on them on the day of Pentecost (see Acts ch. 2). If doubt reigns in the believability and legitimacy of an actual experience of God, rehashing the story (and giving evidence if available) is a necessary component that explains the spiritual encounter did occur.

In Luke 24:13–35, two men on their way to Emmaus were conversing about the extraordinary, and disheartening events that occurred (and dashed all their hopes of a redeemer expected to overpower Roman supremacy) with Jesus' crucifixion in

---

17. Lane, *Experience of God*, 33.

Induction

Jerusalem. The narrative explains further how Jesus joins these beleaguered travelers and conversed with them unfolding the scriptures about the necessity of these events, turning their most troubling moments into comfort and enlightenment. Notwithstanding, Jesus still had to redirect their misguided notion of his divine purpose and mission. It is often the case one's expectancy from God is not congruent with the character and divine purpose of God, particularly when it is motivated by one's own personal hopes and dreams. Apostle Peter, for instance, experienced Jesus on such a profound level and received his counsel, and yet he still stumbled at the purpose of his mission and passion because his expectations of Jesus were not in line with his own desires and messianic expectation (see Matt 16:21–23).

The salient point in the narrative is that Jesus' identity was concealed by God, and not without divine reason. This raises the question what was the purpose of his concealed identity? Surely if the travelers recognized Jesus' true identity, it would have been a moment of jubilation turning their encounter into a worship experience, this experience undoubtedly would confirm Jesus' identity and resurrected body, but this revelation would have derailed the greater import of the journey experience which was indispensable at this particular time. All experiences of God are not the same, and all experiences do not yield the same results, but all experiences of God are timely encounters and not without divine order.

We should be aware that Jesus initiated the experience and closed the experience in which he departs from their presence (once all the necessary revelation was given). After living in such an eye-opening experience in which their hearts burned within (24:32), one would assume nothing else remains, but to walk in the revelation of the experience, and therefore act upon it. Well, this is simply not the case, when one has an experience with God, particularly those worthy of note, the testimonial kind, those that have a message that moves beyond self, the experience with the Divine moves to a different inductive stage. In other words, the experience is not meant to be stored away locked up in a treasure chest and brought out and used only for personal reflection,

Induction and Example

encouragement, and direction; the experience or experiences are intended to encourage and be shared with the community of believers (24:33–35), and to those outside the community of faith, they are meant to testify to the reality of Jesus.

When the eternal God interacts with mortals, it is not simply to say, "Hi, how are you," rather God reveals God's self to initiate an interaction which require a response from the subject.[18] These religious encounters and experiences often come when a person least expects it, and they often interrupt life with its demands, but also come unexpectedly with its joys.[19] In Acts 9:1–19, Paul on (the road to Damascus) his way to further persecute those who belonged to the Way, and without prior warning, Christ interposes and thwarts Paul's crusade to persecute Christians. This religious encounter (whether an inward conversion or call to the Gentiles or both) and the experiences that followed forever changed the trajectory of Paul's life. He became astutely aware of his calling and purpose (no longer as a persecutor of the church, but a proclaimer of it) in which he never relinquished that fervor for Christ. His letters demonstrate that he not only took the mantle for Christ, but ran with it.

Although Paul had a unique revelatory experience with Christ, it was necessary that his experience was affirmed by others (not to affirm his gospel which he would later proclaim to the Gentiles), and this happened under the patronage of God's servant Ananias, who through a vision was instructed to receive and validate Paul's new religious experience.[20] We are reminded without Ananias, Paul's religious experience would only be his, and his alone. He would have wondered in blindness on how to build on that experience. People may indeed have a religious experience outside of community such as Paul, but as Lane explains, it is difficult to critically examine one's own experience and therefore it

---

18. God may simply instruct the person, to do or not to do, to say or not to say, to guide, to direct, to instruct, etc.

19. Lane, *Experience of God*, 27.

20. See also Acts 22:6–16; 26:12–18.

Induction

is essential that they become attached to community.[21] God connected Paul with someone who was already a part of the community of faith in which he was now to join.

To the last point, one's divine encounter with God may not be as high profiled as Paul's Damascus road experience, or even considered a higher calling, but the premise remains the same, one becomes aware of the transcendent and immanence being, in which knowledge of God's grace and nature is disclosed, and one also becomes aware of his or her own spiritual and earthly journey with God.[22] God may simply direct a person to what seminary or college to attend, or God might alert a person of a life situation, or to do something that is beneficial for one's life.

In 2 Cor 12:1–10, Paul pens an extraordinary revelatory experience where he was caught up to the third heaven or paradise and heard and seen unspeakable things, which he was not permitted to share. This ecstatic experience apparently dwelled in the bosom of Paul for his own edifying, he nevertheless reaches back into his treasure trove of religious experiences (fourteen years ago) because he was compelled to address his opponents and his community in Corinth. The super apostles, as Paul calls them, questioned and interrogated the legitimacy of his apostleship simply because his apostolic credentials did not meet their definition of a true apostle: that is, his refusal to accept financial support, his lack of rhetorical skill, and demonstration of signs and wonders.

In v. 7 Paul informs us he experienced other great revelations for which he circumvents the specifics of them. These revelatory experiences were not useless spiritual realities or empty inductive experiences for Paul, they were foundational experiences that enhanced his knowledge of Christ, and ultimately undergirds his relationship with him. This is why Paul had such an incessant dedication to Christ because of the abundance of revelations given

21. Lane, *Experience of God*, 22.

22. Lane explains, "There can be no such thing as a 'pure' experience without reference to some elements of understanding. Experience without understanding is an empty event." However, as T. S. Eliot explains, there are times a person may have had "the experience but missed the meaning." Lane, *Experience of God*, 21.

Induction and Example

him, it groomed his theology, and enabled him to minister with fortitude, testify religiously, and endure innumerable hardships with relentless commitment (see 11:22–29). This should alert the believer if God reveals God's self through various revelations and experiences, and the person is blessed with God's divine favor, and have special gifts and talents, more is demanded and required from that person by God.[23] "To whom much is given much is required." To prevent excessive pride because of these "surpassingly great revelations," a thorn of some kind was given Paul by the same divine source of the revelations sometime after these experiences. This reminds us although Paul was endowed spiritually and exposed to otherworldly experiences, which others would be desirous to experience, he was still flesh and blood susceptible to inordinate pride. The servants of God in all their servicing capacities whether civil, political or religious are not emancipated from a thorny issue if their arrogance of their attainments are lifted up beyond measure.

Even though Paul ask God three times to remove the thorn, in which God denied his request, the permanency of the thorn that weakened his flesh nevertheless brought grace and dependency on God that preserved him throughout his life. There is often a curiosity in knowing the type of thorn that Paul received, but Paul redirects our attention from the propensity to know, and would have us to know what is most important, the grace that was mediated in weakness. Matera adds, "The thorn for the flesh then is the necessary antidote to the super exaltation that accompanies visions and revelations, the constant reminder of Paul's weakness and dependency on Christ."[24] In weakness God's power is fully demonstrated.

---

23. What is required of that person can come in many forms: worship, service, gifts, etc.

24. Matera, 2 *Corinthians*, 284.

Induction

High and Low Probabilities

Induction always involve probability because there is no certainty that there will be a continuous pattern between particular cases. In that regard, induction can be either strong or weak; a strong inductive inference is based on repeated evidence, the more evidence offered increases the probability of the observation or experience being true or likely to happen again. A weak induction provides less confirming evidence (or the likelihood of) an event or experience occurring again, but this does not necessarily negate an experience of the same kind happening again.

The theory of probability can be useful in analyzing biblical passages, and even though the laws of probability are more sophisticated in inductive theory in ancient times than how they are described below, the writers nevertheless overruled the problem of induction, and attached the certainty to their inductive conclusion. One can imagine the residual effect that will occur if everything the Bible states, and the church believes are uncertain, doubt will certainly reign in the believer.

Let us look at a simple case, and a hypothetical one. If God answers a petitioner's prayer on four different and consecutive occasions, this does not prove that God will answer the next prayer with any certainty because anything could interfere with God answering the fifth prayer. For instance, the request may not be in God's will (1 John 5:14), or it may be based on lust (Jas 4:3), lack of faith (Heb 11:6), timing (Rom 8:28; 2 Cor 6:2; Col 4:2), or sin (1 John 1:9), etc. Although the believer's request may go unanswered the next time, this does not preclude that God will not answer the person's prayer in the future.[25] The key element a person's faith would have matured to the point that he or she comes to know God is capable of answering prayers even if God fails to do so the next time. To the Christian believer, faith is the assurance of knowing that God is capable.[26]

---

25. See Matt 7:7.
26. See Heb 11:1–3.

Induction and Example

A more advance case occurs when the author of 2 Pet responds to the uncertainty of Christ's return in 2 Pet 3:4. The verse states, "Where is this coming he promised? Ever since our ancestors died, everything goes on as it has since the beginning of creation." No doubt the scoffers reasoned that time has elapsed and "the course of the world, i.e., of human history and of the physical world in which it is set, has always continued without the catastrophic intervention of divine judgments."[27] Thus the merit of the scoffers' argument is strong since their conclusion rest (and if intended) on Christ's Parousia; arguing that Jesus did not return as promised and anticipated in their generation, so they question his future return. Unless the author can provide concrete examples that God has indeed intervened in the empirical world the scoffers' accusation and argument remains unchallenged. And for the author to respond by saying, Jesus will one day return in the future, and one must have faith is simply inadequate and a useless rebuttal. Thus the author understood the detriment this type of ideology would have on the eschatological hope of the church, and therefore this accusation elicited a firm and powerful response.

Nevertheless, the author demonstrates his knowledge of biblical history, which he shows it is not an issue of uncertainty of Christ's return, but rather his Parousia is based on God's eternal will that any should perish but come to repentance (2 Pet 3:9).[28] Thus he counters their accusation by employing a past example as evidence that God spoke into existence the world which was destroyed previously by water and, in the future, God will judge again by fire (3:6–7). The author reminds the reader's if God who is powerful enough to bring about the first event, surely there is nothing in heaven or below that can impede God from bringing about the second one. So, the question is not about God defaulting on fulfilling the promise rather God's divine purpose and forbearance for mortal beings salvation. Edwin A. Blum explains:

---

27. Senior and Harrington, *1 Peter, Jude and 2 Peter*, 294.

28. In Luke 1:1–3, Luke assures Theophilus of the certainty of Christ's mission and purpose.

Induction

> The fact that the continuance of the world as a stable habitation for mankind has always depended and continues to depend on the will of God. He did destroy the world once by flood. The observable stability of the world is therefore no guarantee of its continued stability in the future; it is being preserved in existence by God only until the time he has appointed for judgment of the wicked.[29]

He assures and informs the readers that Christ's return is designated in God's time and not mortal's opinion. It is also important to note that the Christian community believes ("popular opinion" or "endoxa" among Christians of Christ's Parousia) Christ's delay and return is not predicated on the improbable, but rather of faith and divine assurance in Jesus' resurrection. That one day he will return.

Summary

In the analysis of induction: sense perception, observation and experience are essential elements in learning and knowing the nature of a subject or object. Those individuals in the selected passages often make substantial claims based on their inductive experience. For instance, Jesus understood the nature of flora and fauna by direct observation and as a result of his induction concluded this is what they do. Peter's visionary experience transforms his theology, and Paul's inductive experiences were foundational that molded his dedication to Christ.

---

29. Blum, *1 Peter*, 285.

4

Identifying Biblical Example

IN GRECO-ROMAN ORATORY, SKILLED orators often construct speeches and writings employing the example (Gk. *paradeigma*) to support an argument, one would reasonably think that linguistic indicators such as "for example" or "for instance" would introduce the example, and be a part of the grammatical structure. Skilled orators, however, including Aristotle and many of his successors often focused more on logical structures of arguments than linguistic indicators.[1] In fact, the majority of ancient manuals that write on rhetoric that emphasize example as a rhetorical tool are not using the argumentative connector.[2] Not surprising then, the NT linguistic indicators that introduce the example are also noticeably absence; consequently the interpreter often has to supply the phrase "for example" in front or the middle of a passage to assist in comprehension.[3] In reference to linguistic indicators and

---

1. Eggs and McElholm, *Exemplifications*, 117.
2. Eggs and McElholm, *Exemplifications*, 117.
3. Here are a few examples. In Acts 20:35, Paul states that "in everything I did, I showed [as an example to] you that by this kind of hard work we must help the weak, remembering the words the Lord Jesus himself said: It is more

Identifying Biblical Example

their identification in the biblical corpus, the rhetorical example is only intermittently self-identifiable and made lucid by the author's grammatical markers and sentence construction: word choice, syntax, and context.

In Rom 7:1-2, Paul does not insert the phrase "for example" at the beginning of 7:2 to clarify the statement in 7:1. The contextual evidence that an example is being used is the speaking of the law in the Romans context, to speaking about marriage bond which forms the example.[4] The ushering in of one context that is outside the present context often alerts the reader that an example is being used. Tobin explains the placement of the example in greater detail (7:1-6):

> The cause of this complexity is two. One is the old relationship between the example from Jewish marriage law in 7:2-3 and Paul claims about the effects of the death

---

blessed to give than to receive." In Heb 12:3, the example arises from the exhortation to "consider him [Jesus as an example] who endured such opposition from sinners, so that you will not grow weary and lose heart." In Eph 5:2, the author exhorts the audience to "walk in the way of love, just as Christ loved us [as an example] and gave himself up for us as a fragrant offering and sacrifice to God." In Heb 12:1-2, the author explains that "therefore, since we are surrounded by such a great cloud of witnesses [as our previous exemplars of faith], let us throw off everything that hinders and the sin that so easily entangles, and let us run with perseverance the race marked out for us, looking to Jesus, [as our example] the founder and perfecter of our faith, who for the joy that was set before him endured the cross, despising the shame, and is seated at the right hand of the throne of God." In Titus 1:11, the author contends that "they must be silenced, because they are [bad examples] disrupting whole households by teaching things they ought not to teach—and that for the sake of dishonest gain." In Matt 23:3, the author argues "you must be careful to do everything they tell you. But do not do what they do, [because they are bad examples] for they do not practice what they preach." In 1 Tim 1:20, the author points out that "among them are Hymenaeus and Alexander [are negative examples of the faith], whom I have handed over to Satan to be taught not to blaspheme." It is of note that these examples are not necessarily rhetorical, these exhortations demonstrate that the phrase "for example" need to be inserted to understand the purpose of the example.

4. The phrase does not appear in the original Greek text. The New International Version translators do apply "for example" in (7:2) to augment comprehension, but not all translations apply the phrase.

Induction and Example

and resurrection of Christ on believers and their relationship to the Mosaic Law in 7:4-6. The other is Paul's complex interpretation of Christ's death and resurrection and their consequences for believers in 7:4-6 itself. First the example taken from Jewish marriage in 7:2-3, the wife is bound . . . the emphasis is on the change in the woman's legal status due to her husband's death. But in the principle that Paul enunciates in 7:1 and that the example is presumably meant to illustrate, the emphasis is elsewhere. "The law has power over a person as long as the person is alive" the principle in 7:1 in fact applies to the situation of the husband who dies, whereas the example in 7:2-3 is about the situation of the wife who is still alive. . . . In addition, it is the principle rather than the example that Paul develops in 7:4-6. In relationship to the example in 7:2-3, believers are in the position of the husband and not the wife. . . . What role, then, does the example from Jewish marriage law play in 7:1-6? Its role is twofold. First, since he is appealing, perhaps with a bit of irony, to the Roman Christians as "those who know the law can cease to have force when death occurs. In spite of all the dissimilarities between 7:1, 4-6 and the example in 7:2-3, the point of similarities is this. Death can bring about the cessation of the binding force of a law. Second and more important, one needs to see Paul's use of the example from Jewish marriage law against the background of the rather different way he wrote earlier about the cessation of the binding force of the Mosaic law on believers.[5]

If this line of argument has a semblance of truth, Paul must have thought his readers would be able to navigate through these lengthy and integrated paradeigmata and comprehend how they are to be applied to their context. Thus, the readers must actively participate in understanding the usage of the example otherwise the example fails to communicate meaning and purpose.

---

5. Tobin, *Romans*, 220-21.

Identifying Biblical Example

The Contextual Example

The general meaning or the etymology of the "word exemplum [Latin] is akin to the verb eximere, 'to take out, to remove, to take away, to free,' to make an exception of. Therefore, the example is something cut out and removed from some whole."[6] Thus the example is not a proof that exists as an independent unit or in isolation from other texts, but rather is a part of a whole. The example depends on its immediate and larger context (which introduces the example) for meaning and interpretation.[7] Although the interpreter may seize the rudimentary meaning of a self-contained example, this does not disclose the rational for including the example. Interpreters often misinterpret and decontextualize example text because they analyze the proof on its own terms without properly considering its dependency.

There are several reasons why an author may employ an example.[8] I will only explore three: (1) the author may use example(s) to support his propositio; (2) the example may be used to support a sub-propositio or even smaller topics in the biblical text; and (3) the example used as an illustration.

The Historical Example

Jane D. Chaplin explains the famous oration of Marcus Furius Camillus, she concludes, "Aiming to persuade the Romans not to abandon their city, which they have just won back from the Gauls, Camillus argues against moving to Veii. His speech, which

---

6. Lyons, *Exemplum*, 9.
7. Harvey, *Exemplarity and the Origins of Legislation*, 251–54.
8. Cicero asserts that examples can be used: (1) To persuade the audience (De inventione. 1.6). (2) Aesthetically "it is simply a pleasure to listen to reference to the past, and a happy audience is the easier convinced (Cic. Orator 1.20.66)." (3) They have a moral didactic purpose "as he discusses the ways in which an exemplum can be used to teach a lesson and can inspire men to imitate the great deeds of the ancestors (Cic.Arch.14; De or.2.36.2.355)." (4) To console those in grief (Tusculanae Disputationes 3.58). Blom, *Cicero's Role Models*, 66–68.

Induction and Example

revolves the sanity of Rome and its location, uses exempla to support many points."[9] Aristotle also states the purpose of a historical paradeigma in the *Rhetoric to Alexander*:

> *Examples* are actions that have taken place that are similar or contrary to those being discussed by us now. You must use them whenever what you are saying is hard to believe but you want to make clear (if it does not become credible through an argument from plausibility) that once they learn that an action similar to the one being discussed by you has been done as you say it was done, they will believe more in what you are saying.[10]

Aristotle emphasizes that historical examples are useful when an rhetor is unable to prove his case. If a person, for instance, is unable to argue convincingly to a skeptical group of people that global warming is a real issue, Aristotle recommends that the person employ paradeigmata showing how climate change has deteriorated the environment in the past, and the same type of environmental issues will continue to accelerate if changes are not made in the future. Thus the hearers will be better disposed to believe your argument because the paradeigmata substantiates your case.

As a new movement within Judaism, the new developing (Christian) community would search "the scriptures to find just the right example, maxim, proverb, oracle, or legal precedents for a given argument."[11] They often searched within their own Judaic history for well-known instead of lesser-known historical and milestone events such as the exodus experience and the giving of the law, and more notably the deeds of venerated figures, namely, Adam, Noah, the patriarchs, and the prophets. When the biblical writer employs historical paradeigmata they are not meant to narrate history, but rather the writer ushers in the past because they are part of his discourse and rhetorical agenda, and to guide the audience course of action in the future.

---

9. Chaplin, *Livy's Exemplary History*, 86.
10. Aristotle, *Rhet. Alex.* 8.
11. Mack, *Rhetoric and the New Testament*, 32.

Identifying Biblical Example

In Heb 11:3-40, the author employs an extensive but selective list of historical examples of faithful individuals, each example is introduced by the key phrase "by faith," which explains how these heroic figures were able to accomplish daring deeds and noteworthy acts. We should be aware first off these historical examples are weaved into the narrative world, and should be understood as part of a whole. Michael Cosby points out, "So similar is the language in 12:1-13 to that of 10:19-39 that, if the mention of the great cloud of witnesses in 12:1-13 were omitted, all of Hebrews 11 could be left out and the sermon would proceed quite smoothly."[12] The reason behind the inclusion of the examples in Hebrew 11:3-40 can be traced to the introduction 11:1-2 and reaches further back to the exhortation 10:19-39.[13] In each individual example, or the example list, the author wishes to encourage the readers and auditors to remain steadfast in the midst of persecution and trials. The author was not trying to deduce through rigorous statements on why the community should remain faithful, the author simply depends on the past to speak to the present, and to encourage and strengthen their faith in the future. Thus, the example is not useless proofs, but rather a powerful rhetorical mechanism the author uses to establish and promote enduring faith.

In Jas 2:21-26, the author ushers in the patriarch Abraham and Rahab as historical paradeigmata, to attest that genuine faith is not detached from works but partnered with works. These examples are not dangling in the narrative without purpose, they are employed solely to support the author's proposition in the present. Donald W. Burdick explains, "(2:14-26) divides itself into three sections: the proposition (vv. 14-17); the argument (vv. 18-25); and the concluding statement (v. 26)."[14] I would like to reroute this structure, however, the proposition only reaches back to v. 14. The author's hypothetical albeit rhetorical question is answered, and illustrated by giving a short example of a brother or sister being

---

12. Cosby, *Rhetorical Composition and Function*, 85.
13. Cosby, *Rhetorical Composition and Function*, 26.
14. Burdick, *James*, 182.

Induction and Example

destitute vv. 15–17. In vv. 18–20, he explains his reasoning further, but it is not until 2:21–23 that he ushers in the examples.

In the primary example (2:21–23), Abraham "The patriarch's faith could not be so adequately designated unless and until he demonstrated it by what he did in obedience to God who justifies him . . . it was a faith that needed to come to expression by his deeds."[15] In other words, Abraham's faith did not function in isolation apart from works, but his faith worked and was proven to be authentic when he attempted to offer Isaac as a sacrifice (Gen 15:6–22). In the secondary example (2:25), Rahab's faith was confirmed by her actions, in which "she chose to become identified with the people of Israel, a decision based on faith (cf. Josh 2:8–13; Heb 11:31). Far from being dead or worthless, her faith moved her to risk her life to protect the spies."[16] It is important to bear in mind that the recognition and admiration of Abraham's faith in Jewish history is potent enough to communicate exemplification on its own, without the need of Rahab's example. Rahab's example, which is not expressed in great detail, is only compulsory to reinforce the primary example of Abraham. Both examples nevertheless are rhetorical and fall under the same class to demonstrate that genuine faith proves to be faithful when accompanied by works.

In addition, Burdick states that "James does not imply that deeds are the actual life principle that gives life to faith, but only that faith and deeds are inseparable. If there are no acts springing from faith, that faith is no more alive than the 'body without the spirit.'"[17] Under this premise, James is not arguing how salvation is acquired, nor is he offending Paul's theology of justification by faith, rather he simply explains how faith and works coexist and are inseparable illustrated by the examples.

---

15. Martin, *James*, 92.
16. Burdick, *James*, 185.
17. Burdick, *James*, 185.

Identifying Biblical Example

Discovery of Historical Examples

Aristotle contends the historical example is more difficult to discover than the analogy and fable are because the example requires a diligent search for events that have similar characteristics to the case under discussion.[18] Birger Gerhardsson adds that "it is not the mere reporting or arbitrary discoveries of an event or persons of the past that makes it persuasive and convincing, but the discovery of the analogical and generalizations."[19] Therefore the rhetor does not discover any type of example and try to make it fit contextually, rather the rhetor starts with what brought the present crisis into existence, and then discovers the type of historical example to be used. Needless to say, it is the responsibility of the rhetor to secure the temperament of the audience, and understand their social, political, and cultural background, and knowing whether the audience has knowledge of the example. This information will determine how the example is structured and formed.

To another point, the example is not interchangeable fitting neatly into every context but rather fitted for a certain context.[20] If we examine each example Paul employs in Galatians, particularly in chs. 1–2 and 3:6–9, they are contextually controlled and governed by the incidents that took place in Galatia. To assign Paul's examples in Galatians and reconstitute the same examples in Corinthians or even Philippians would decontextualize the examples because the theology, the causation of the events, the social situation, and the rhetoric of each epistle are different. There is one exception, the examples used in Galatians and Romans are applicable because both letters deal with the law and faith, as well as Abraham as a personal and historical example. Thomas Tobin explains that "Paul makes much the same point in using the example of Abraham and quoting Gen 15:6 in Rom 4:3 as he did in Gal 3:6, that is, that Abraham was made righteous by God because of

---

18. Aristotle, *Rhet.* 2.20.8.
19. Gerhardsson, *Memory and Manuscript*, xxxv.
20. Harvey, "Exemplarity and the Origins of Legislation," 249.

Induction and Example

his faith and not because of his observance of the law."[21] The main difference nevertheless is that the examples used in Galatians are shaped around the truth of the gospel: Christian liberty and how Gentiles are identified. This is not the case in Romans.

In Jas 5:11, the author employs Job as a historical example that exemplify enduring patience. Instead of reflecting on the book that reflects his name, as one who ask God for an explanation, and complained of his suffering and misfortunes, and one who did not exhibit patience in the midst of trials, the author discovers and chooses the patience of Job (as a faithful believer who persevered despite the calamities) that was developed during the intertestamental period.[22] His depiction of Job in these writings were more in line with his argumentative and persuasive strategy of persevering, in the hope that his community will take on the same pattern of behavior by persevering through hardships. The canonical Job still had faith in God.[23] Therefore the example was not to teach a Bible lesson on what it means to be patience under duress, but to address real issues and taxing experiences that needed immediate attention. The example is meant to guide the community's attitude and behavior in the future.

As we examine the text rhetorically, we are alerted that the example has two layers. First, the author brings the audience into the immediate awareness of the example, by stating, "You have heard of Job's perseverance."[24] This rhetorical technique enables the community to cooperate in Job's perseverance within the framework of their own. This shared experience of suffering in the midst of trials allows the community to continue to identify with Israel's past, in which they will be better disposed to embrace hardship knowing the prophets and Job endured adversity, and therefore they can too. Second, James explains (the main crux of the example) the outcome of Job's experience, which he concludes his twofold statement you

21. Tobin, *Paul's Rhetoric in Its Contexts*, 147.
22. Hartin, *James*, 256.
23. Martin, *James*, 194. See Job chs. 10 and 23.
24. I will only use the New International Version of the Bible as a translation throughout the book.

Identifying Biblical Example

"have seen what the Lord finally brought about." He emboldens the community to see the means (through endurance) by which God's grace and mercy will carry you through. Patrick J. Hartin explains, "The outcome of Job's endurance was the reward God gave Job by restoring his life and former fortunes because he had remained faithful."[25] The focus therefore is to exhort the community the best course of action to achieve those ends if they remain faithful. All those who persevere to the end will be called blessed.

In 2 Pet 2:1–10, the author discovers four historical examples to condemn the false teachers (and their behavior) who bring false doctrines and heresies like the false prophets of old that distort the truth, the narrative also explains how God is able to rescue the godly out of trials. These examples sets the pattern from which the author argues, and we must note unless a pattern of behavior and events are edged in stone, or history, the author has nothing to base his current argument.[26] With that being said, the examples are contrastic in nature: (A) The sinful angels who were divinely judged, (B) the righteous Noah who God preserved, (A) the divine judgment and destruction of the wicked cites Sodom and Gomorrah, (B) and the preservation of Lot. Each contrastic example reinforces the pattern of the other, but each example is of no greater strength than the other. Thus the examples are of equal value because class (A) represent divine judgment and class (B) represent divine rescuing.

The first example of the fallen angels in the Book of Watchers come from a noncanonical Jewish source. This was not a fanciful story that had no origin, but was rooted in early Jewish history that explains how particular historical events transpired (the credibility of the story made its way into the biblical canon: 2 Peter and Jude). If the events were perceived as imaginary, they would present obstacles from which to draw truth. We stated earlier in chapter 2 that King Agrippa's speech to the Jews was persuasive because the historical examples he used were built on truth. Nevertheless,

---

25 Hartin, *James*, 256.

26. An author may, however, exhort an audience to go against a pattern in history.

Induction and Example

"in the Book of the Watchers (1 En. 1–36) as an elaboration of the story of the sons of God of Gen 6:1–4. In the Watcher tradition, the sons of God are understood to be angels. They mate with human women who give birth to sons, the giants. The giants are exceedingly evil and, together with their supernatural fathers, lead the whole world astray, thus precipitating the flood. In this respect and in contrast to Gen 3, this unnatural union, rather than the fall of Adam, becomes the chief cause of evil in the world (1 En. 10:8–10)."[27] The relevance and import of the example is that "the mention of angels that sinned in 2 Pet 2:4 appears in the context of a warning against false teachers who would come into the flock (2:1–22)."[28] Since all historical examples are rhetorical and designed to persuade or dissuade a person or community in the future, this future judgment (albeit a harsh indictment) was not permanent because they still had an opportunity to repent of their heretical teaching and behavior. If they could see what is coming perhaps this would change their ways.

The second example of Noah is recorded in Genesis where God instructs him to build an ark; for the sole purpose to save him and seven others from the deluge. The author did not attempt to capture every aspect of Noah's history such as, the covenant God made with him promising not to destroy the world again with water nor did he try to capture the exemplary faith and patience of Noah or his actions after the flood. If all these aspects were added the readers would have become lost in the cloud of the example trying to figure out the analogy between the past and present.[29] The author was selective and narrows down one aspect in which he seeks Noah as a preacher of righteousness whom God protects. Scott Hafemann adds, "At the narrative level, Yhwh is the one who both closes the door from the outside to seal Noah in the ark (Gen 7:16) and tells him to come out after the flood is over (Gen 8:16),

---

27. Papaioannou, "Sin of the Angels," 393.
28. Papaioannou, "Sin of the Angels," 399.
29. The author did mention the flood narrative in 2 Pet 3, but he shaped the example around the scoffer's argument.

Identifying Biblical Example

thereby emphasizing, as in 2 Pet 2:–10a, that God is the one who protects God's righteous servant."[30]

The third example are the wicked cities Sodom and Gomorrah. The wickedness and immoral behavior of these two cities God pronounced judgment and destroyed. The judgment of these cities in Genesis were not without prior warning Gen 18–20. At the request of Abraham, God would spare the city if any righteous inhabitants were discovered. Ryan P. Juza adds, "The striking implication is that God was willing to pardon the whole for the sake of a part. Thus, we can infer that God's desire was that everyone be saved (not perish). His willingness to reduce the number from 50 to 10 demonstrates this fact, but certain conditions needed to be met. He needed to find righteous people in S & G."[31] The account of Sodom and Gomorrah in Genesis describe a temporal judgment without any regard to their eschatological future, but the story had eventually "developed its own tradition in subsequent literature. It was understood as a prototype for divine judgment of the ungodly, and by the time of the NT it was being used eschatologically."[32] Thus the author uses this tradition rhetorically to address the ungodly in his eschatological community in hopes of drawing repentance.

The fourth example of Lot. Although conflated with the third example of Sodom and Gomorrah, the emphasis here is on how God spared Lot and his family. Like the example of Noah, the author had no interest in making known the complete history of Lot such as, his gracious act of hospitality in which he invited two angels into his home, or to document the disbelief of his son-in-law's of the coming doom of the city, or Lot's wife being turned into a pillar of salt, rather the author focuses on Lot's righteousness. Juza explains that the author "comments on the devastating nature of its fiery destruction as an example (2:6), on how God rescued the righteous man Lot (2:7), and on the torment experienced by Lot as a result of witnessing the ungodly behavior of those around him

---

30. Hafemann, "Noah, the Preacher of (God's) Righteousness," 313.
31. Juza, "Echoes of Sodom and Gomorrah," 234.
32. Juza, "Echoes of Sodom and Gomorrah," 229–30.

(2:8)."[33] Thus the key point the author wishes to demonstrate is how God rescued Lot and Noah, and can do the same for godly in his community.

To summarize: The foundation of each example is rooted in God's infinite wisdom to bring an event to pass, and is all-powerful to rescue the godly out of trials. Each example is prefaced with "if God" is able. The author's rhetoric is, if God is able (Noah is also implied) to rescue and protect Noah and Lot, which both serve as "positive counterpart to the sinful angels, the ungodly ancient world, and the notorious cities of Sodom and Gomorrah, all of which suffered God's judgment (2 Pet 2:5–8),"[34] God is certainly able to rescue and protect the godly from trials in his community. And if God is able to protect those individuals from such trials, surely God is able to rescue the righteous in future generations. And if God is able to hold judgment for the unrighteous in the past, surely God is able to do the same for those individuals in the future. If God remains immutable in nature and being, it only follows that God still has the power to protect the godly and bring certain events to past.

Reinterpreting the Historical Example

The historical example is always open to reinterpretation by the orator, who controls the meaning and application of these events and persons. It is not the orator's purpose to rewrite history the interpreter only seeks to reinterpret the example for a brand new audience. The past and present are orchestrated by the orator, but the future decision always remains in the hands of the target audience. In the NT age, the OT authors no longer possessed or controlled the meaning of the Hebrew Scriptures but these newly endowed NT exegetes did. These authors retold Israel's experiences and traditions, but also became interpreters of that history and ultimately determined how the event or persons actions should be applied. In

---

33. Juza, "Echoes of Sodom and Gomorrah," 231.
34. Hafemann, "Noah, the Preacher of (God's) Righteousness," 106.

Identifying Biblical Example

other words, the NT authors "were not trying to say what the text used to mean before the advent of Christ. What would be the point of that? Rather, they were trying to interpret the ancient texts given what they now know and what they have now experienced."[35] The old story was lifted from its original setting and becomes the foundation for an entirely new setting and context.

In 2 Cor 3:14–15, Paul ushers in this rather complex narrative of the veiling of Moses' face in the wilderness and reinterprets this experience to address the community in Corinth. He contends the veil before, still continues "even to this day when Moses is read, a veil covers their hearts" (3:15). What exactly does Paul mean? Steve Moyise explains:

> Indeed, to this very day whenever Moses is read, a veil lies over their minds; but when one turns to the Lord, the veil is removed. The purpose of the veil in the original story (Exodus 34) was to prevent the people seeing Moses' glowing face. It was not simply "sunblock" to dull the image but a "covering" to hide Moses' face. And when Paul switches to discussing the reading of Moses, he says that that same veil lies over their minds. In other words, they cannot see what is there until they turn to the Lord and the veil is taken away.[36]

Out of the plethora of experiences that Paul could choose from the Moses context, he abstracts only the purpose behind the veil, and this is for rhetorical reasons. So, whether Moses knew of the coming of a new covenant of the Spirit is inapplicable in the new context, because what matters most to Paul is that both the Jews of Moses' day and the Jews of his day remain in blindness until they come to the Lord. The common factor is that both narratives belong to the same class of covering of the veil, which (caused blindness or hardiness of the heart) makes the analogy applicable in a new context.

In Gal 4:21–31, the pericope by Paul's own admission is categorized as an allegory, some scholars even interpret it typologically,

---

35. Moyise, *Use of Analogy in Biblical Studies*, 35.
36. Moyise, *Use of Analogy in Biblical Studies*, 35.

Induction and Example

but despite the echoes of these readings in the text, I elect to say, the narrative functions equally as a historical example because the narrative cites real historical figures and places of the past for rhetorical reasons,[37] and therefore they are meant to persuade the Galatians to accept the truth of the gospel. The example is employed to effectively argue his position in Gal 1:6–9, 10–12. Here Paul advances these historical characters of (Isaac and Sarah—free; Ishmael and Hagar—slave) and places (Mt. Sinai and Jerusalem from below and Jerusalem from above) as figures of contrast. There exist a platform of binary oppositions between these characters and spaces. The point Paul wants the Galatians to understand is that "those who believe the promise of God in Christ, are heirs like the children of the free woman Sarah. The opponents (or Jews) are compared to the children of the slave woman Hagar who were born according to the flesh."[38] Thus, the Galatians are required to make a judgment between alternatives, one provided by God (Paul's gospel) and the other by man (the agitators' false gospel).

Recent or Present Examples

The present or recent example may occur within the proximity of the current situation or even several years or decades apart from it. Quintilian recommends that the orator be supplied with examples not only recorded in history, but also recent ones and those that occur day to day.[39] The question may arise, however, is there an advantage of employing a present paradeigma over and against a historical one? Indeed! One particular advantage is that it may be "better known to the audience."[40] The reader and auditor may have firsthand awareness of the event allowing them to actively engage in the paradeigma, enabling them to acknowledge and verify the truth of the event, or the falsity of it. Another advantage is the

---

37. See Price, "Παραδειγμα and Exemplum," 40–41.
38. Loubser, "Contrast Slavery/Freedom," 164.
39. Quintilian, *Inst.* 12.4.1.
40. Blom, *Cicero's Role Models*, 115.

Identifying Biblical Example

orator is not necessarily enmeshed with describing the event in great detail which one may have with using a historical example.

When Jesus taught the parable of the Friend at midnight, the auditors were immediately aware of the cultural milieu that embodied the parable Luke 11:5–8. He grabbed their attention by presenting a (hypothetical) question based on the common practice (and historically grounded) of hospitality in the ancient Near East. Alan F. Johnson states:

> Can you imagine having a guest and going to a neighbor to borrow bread and the neighbor offers ridiculous excuses about a locked door and sleeping children?" The Near Eastern listener responds, "No, I cannot imagine such a thing!" Under no circumstances would he fail to get up and leave his friend's request unanswered.[41]

The inductive example has two layers. The first layer. What makes this illustration applicable is the knowledge the auditors had of the cultural and social practices in the first century, and therefore it was not outside their common experience. The audience could not argue against the judiciousness of the parable nor set aside the communal obligation and practice of hospitality that governed the cultural climate. On the basis thereof, Jesus uses this knowledge in which he manipulates cultural and social consciousness that precipitated a positive response. He does not leave room where one can negotiate multiple conclusions, but rather the only conclusion one can induce from the parable.

The second layer. In order for the example to work, however, it must first do its part as a communal and cultural guide Jesus wishes to convey about being persistent in prayer. In other words, Jesus uses the example of the friend at midnight rhetorically, and for no other reason to increase understanding and to make known what is means to be resolute in prayer. Norval Geldenhuys also explains:

> If even an imperfect human being, notwithstanding the inconvenience to which he is put, will arise at midnight to give a friend what he needs if he comes and asks him for

---

41. Johnson, "Assurance for Man," 124.

Induction and Example

> help, how much more will God, the heavenly friend, who is perfect in love, listen to the sincere prayers and supplications of His children who are really in need! It is important that we should remember that in the parable there is a friendship existing between the one who asks and the one who rises and gives, and that the request arises out of necessity and not out of selfishness. The answer to prayer is, therefore, only certain in cases where the one who prays stands in a relation of friendship towards God.[42]

We should also state, Jesus could have easily made statements and gave an explanation on why one should be persistent in prayer, but he uses an illustration instead to drive home his point more forcefully. Examples are employed and meant to open the door for more knowledge, understanding, and as a guide to a greater truth. If perhaps for some reason the audience were unable to comprehend the example of the friend at midnight and the meaning behind it, it is uncertain they would have been able to grasp the truth of being persistence in prayer.

In 1 Cor 12:12–30, Paul begins to explain the ontology of the human body with a major twist, he employs a preexistent body analogy that was a part of the Greek culture. D. B. Martin explains:

> That Paul's imagery is at variance with usual use of such imagery. Instead of using it to support an existing social hierarchy where the lesser members of society serve the greater, Paul uses it to relativize the sense of self-importance of those of higher status, making them see the importance and necessity of the weaker, lower- status, Corinthian Christians.[43]

Thus Paul transmutes this typical social construct (body analogy), which has no rhetorical significance here in the present context. He artistically manipulates this human anatomy to address the ongoing schisms and the superiority complex of individuals who plagued the unity of the Corinthians church, see 1 Cor 7–11, also the proposition 1:10. Herbert M. Gale also explains:

42. Geldenhuys, *Gospel of Luke*, 324–25.
43. Witherington, *Conflict and Community in Corinth*, 259.

Identifying Biblical Example

> Apparently those who possessed the "gift" [of speaking in tongues] were assuming an attitude of superiority over those who did not. Conversely, those who did not possess the gift were inclined to feel that they lacked something that they ought to have if they were to share fully in the Christian life and experience. Paul's purpose in writing was, in part, to convince the Corinthian community that the various Christians, regardless of the gifts that individually might be theirs, must understand the proper place and function of these gifts both in relationship to the larger Christian community and also in relationship to one another. It is in connection with this objective that he introduces the analogy of the human body. The analogy is employed, therefore, (1) to reinforce the idea of unity in diversity, and (2) to indicate the proper relationship between the various factors in the diversity.[44]

Paul would have them know, regardless of the diversity of gifts and talents that the community possesses, all members are one and not above the other; each body part is not only self-serving and distinct, but reliant on one another. Only simple reflection was required to apprehend the cooperative and diverse nature of the human anatomy.

In Rev 2:13, Antipas—who was martyred in Pergamum for his faithful witness—was employed as a present example not to pronounce the unfortunate death of one who died or one who did not surrender to idolatrous behavior, rather the author uses him to persuade believers to remain faithful to Christ in the midst of persecution (albeit not widespread), even if their faithfulness would lead to death. It is to their advantage eschatologically if they "are willing to face physical death with the assurance that eternal life is a gift of God for those who remain faithful."[45] To remain faithful despite the obstacles is the primary aim of the apocalyptist.

The author employs Antipas as a present example as opposed to an ancient one, for which he could have used a martyred prophet of the OT, such as Zechariah, 2 Chr 24:20–22; Matt 23:35; or

---

44. Gale, *Use of Analogy in the Letters of Paul*, 116–17.
45. Kraybill, *Apocalypse and Allegiance*, 37.

Induction and Example

even John the Baptist, Mark 6:14–29; who both were put to death for the cause of God. He selects to use the Antipas example for rhetorical purposes because the auditors could instantly identify with him; not only because his death occurred in their lifetime and would have resonated in their community, but he was a part of their shared experience and ongoing struggle against idolatry and social and economic injustice. An example is only as effective and persuasive as the author's explanation of it, and ultimately how the example communicate meaning and affects the audience's reality. This otherwise unknown person (Antipas) has become known in the Christian canon by John's exemplification of him as a present and personal *paradeigma*.

In 1 Cor 11:17–22, Paul uses a paradeigma, συνερχομένων, or "come together," that describes the sociological effects of division within community over table fellowship initiated from an oral report, ἀκούω or "I hear" (1 Cor 11:18). The example is a subtopic of disunity governed by Paul's *causa* in 1:10.[46] The example shows how discord and conflict threatens the community by making social distinctions between private and public meals, the rich and the poor or the haves and the have nots. Mitchell explains:

> These *schismata*, "factions," are the subject of the *prosthesis* to the argument in 1.10. Because the factions within the church community have been Paul's major concern throughout to this point, there is nothing odd about their "reappearance" here. They have never stopped being of prime importance in the argument. What is often ignored is that in 11:18 the emphasis is not on the fact that *schismata* exist . . . but the fact that these *schismata* are evidence when you come together in assembly. Thus far in his letter Paul has dealt with manifestations of community disunity and strife which takes place in the

---

46. Scholars are in disagreement as to whether disunity is a result of (1:10–12) or if it is a separate division. Gordon D. Fee believes this is not a reflection of the same reality; this division is not based on "quarrels" and "jealousy." He also states "this section does not address anti-Paul in quarrelling." Fee, *First Epistle to the Corinthians*, 537.

Identifying Biblical Example

arena of relations among Christians within the larger social context of the city of Corinth.[47]

Although this example is within the context of social inequality, it is one of the incidents that demonstrates a far greater problem in Corinth because it explains the type of discord that existed from the very beginning in the Corinthian church.

Personal Example

Many ancient authors refer to their own persona as a guide for moral instructions. The Letter of Seneca and Pliny demonstrate self-reference motifs are not an anomaly nor are they described as an eccentric writing style, but are appropriate to employ when one has a greater agenda that moves beyond self.[48] Cicero often presents himself as an exemplary orator, politician and statesmen to establish his own credibility among the Roman elite, and to provide a lasting legacy in the history of ancient Rome.[49] Thus, an orator who employs himself in a speech or writing would become "a natural paradeigma, because the moral character of the orator is an important part of the proof."[50] The orator could also employ examples other than himself, those worthy of imitation and those worthy of avoidance.[51]

Not unexpectedly, the NT is inundated with virtuous and immoral examples of various kinds; i.e., examples of good and bad leaders. It should be pointed out first that although the usage of a person's actions implies an example of some sort, not all moral or unethical examples are rhetorical.[52] The example becomes rhetorical

---

47. Mitchell, *Paul and the Rhetoric of Reconciliation*, 151–52.
48. Gaventa, "Galatians 1 and 2," 323.
49. Blom, *Cicero's Role Models*, 322.
50. Mitchell, *Paul and the Rhetoric of Reconciliation*, 46.
51. Chaplin, *Livy's Exemplary History*, 1.
52. A non-rhetorical example includes: In 1 Cor 11:1, although Paul exhorts the Corinthians to imitate his behavior, as he imitates Christ, the exhortation is not rhetorical. Paul is not attempting to persuade the Corinthian's of anything; they are not faced with alternative choices or encouraged to make a decision in

Induction and Example

when the author employs himself or someone else as rhetorical proofs (logos, ethos and pathos). The identification and usage of paradeigma is to persuade or dissuade the current community of a particular position in the future or when a choice needs to be made between alternatives. It is not simply a case of how a person is an example of courageousness, but how the author is using that courageous person to persuade others to be more courageous.

There are two types of examples observed and should be measured in the NT: (1) those who classify themselves as examples and are recognized as such in the community; and (2) those authors who refer to someone other than themselves as an exemplary figure.[53] Outside of Christ, Paul is recognized as an exemplary biblical figure, who often exhorts others to follow his example.[54] One reason Paul exhorts and calls the new developing community to imitate his example is because:

---

the future, he simply exhorts the Corinthian's to follow his example. In 1 Tim 1:15–16, Paul identifies himself as a paradeigma of the worst of sinners who received mercy and grace. In v. 16, Paul states, "But for that very reason I was shown mercy so that in me, the worst of sinners, Christ Jesus might display his immense patience as an example for those who would believe in him and receive eternal life." Paul was able to speak as a beneficiary and representative of God's grace and mercy because he experienced God's gracious acts firsthand. Although Paul classifies himself as an example, he does not attempt to persuade the community of anything, and thus the example does not function rhetorically. In 2 Tim 1:15–18, although Phygelus and Hermogenes are negative examples and Onesiphorus and his household are positive examples, nothing in the text suggests the examples are rhetorical. In Acts 5:1–11, "Ananias and Sapphira, both husband and wife, are examples of those who violate the integrity of community by the consumption of greed and duplicity." Witherington, *Acts of the Apostles*, 216. This narrative can be classified as an example, but it does not function rhetorically. The author simply tells a story of the events of the early church. In Matt 1:19, Joseph's unwillingness to make Mary a public example speaks to his righteous character but the narrative does not function rhetorically.

53. For an extensive treatment of personal examples, see Benjamin Fiore on the function of personal examples in the Epistles, particularly the Pastorals.

54. Obviously Jesus identifies himself as a majestic exemplum (I am the light of the world, John 8:12). He is identified as a majestic exemplum in the Gospels, Acts of the Apostles, Epistles, and the Apocalypse of John.

Identifying Biblical Example

New converts cannot be expected to have mastered the demands of their new faith and the practices needed to live in accord with these demands in their day to day lives. Such converts will need both instruction in their new faith and concrete examples of how to embody their faith in the various contexts in which they find themselves. . . . It would have been futile for Paul simply to repeat to the Philippians, for example, the abstract command "live a cruciform life." Without giving this phrase some concrete content by pointing to his own life and practice, Paul infers that the Philippians would have been unclear about how to embody such a command. In fact, failure to understand just this aspect of the life of a disciple led some Philippians Christians to succumb to wrong-headed notions, presumably while claiming to live faithfully before Christ. It appears that the Philippians needed to be directed to a concrete example of what a cruciform life might look like in their context if they were to have any expectation of achieving this themselves.[55]

As pastor and founder of several churches, Paul is the logical and natural choice to be an example, and no one else to these new communities.[56]

The second type of example is when an author refers to someone other than himself as an exemplary figure. This type of example any person can essentially become a personal paradigm because an author can turn a reasonable unknown person into a historical or personal example simply by evoking that person's actions and deeds. An overview of Cicero's work demonstrates that people from different socioeconomic, political, and religious backgrounds are suitable personal paradigms.[57] But the most effective and dominant individuals Cicero employs are the Roman elite.[58]

In Rev 2:20, Jezebel is an example of someone who teaches the church in Thyatira to commit fornication and eat foods sacrificed

---

55. Fowl, "Imitation of Paul of Christ," 430.
56. See 1 Cor 4:16; Phil 3:17; 4:9.
57. Blom, *Cicero's Role Models*, 77.
58. Blom, *Cicero's Role Models*, 77.

Induction and Example

to idols. She influenced some of John's community to adopt idolatrous practices through a subterfuge spirituality, in which she steered them to acculturate into the Roman imperial cult. In order for Jesus to illustrate the degree of her deception, and the punishment she will incur if she fails to repent, he reaches back in Israel's history and discovers a relevant example of Jezebel that is in line with his rhetoric.[59] Brian Blount points out that "the first Jezebel was immortalized as the manipulative foreign wife of the Israelite king Ahab. The queen used her influence to prop up her native Baal cult, discredit and destroy the prophets of Yahweh, and lead the people idolatrously astray."[60] It seems certain that she was given the infamous name Jezebel because she demonstrated the same type of influential and misleading behavior as the Jezebel of the past.

The rhetorical aim of the (personal and historical) example is for her, and her disciples, to acknowledge their iniquitous behavior, and turn from their deceitful ways, but the greater reason is to illustrate what would happen if she, and those who follow her continue to engage in unacceptable worship, cultural, and social practices. Jesus explains explicitly, "So I will cast her on a bed of suffering, and I will make those who commit adultery with her suffer intensely, unless they repent of her ways (2:22)." If Jesus gave her a certain amount of time for introspection, or perhaps a rational explanation was given beforehand on why repentance (change behavior) is warranted and this too comes without success; an alternative method to produce conviction and repentance is through a similar experience of the past. In other words, if she failed to take the opportunity to repent and avoid the consequences thereof, the next and last option, however, is to scare her and those who follow using a rhetoric to induce fear. They are surely reminded of the end result of the story of Jezebel which the prophet forecast (and did come to past) that she will encounter a dreadful death by being thrown out of a window, and a pack of devouring dogs would eat away her corpse, and although the Jezebel of the present will not incur such a horrific death, she too will meet her fate by laying in

---

59. See 1 Kgs 18:19—19:3; 2 Kgs 9:7–37.
60. Blount, *Revelation*, 63.

Identifying Biblical Example

a bed of suffering.[61] Thus, Jesus attempts to grab their attention and guide their future behavior by ushering in the past Jezebel, in which he was willing to make her a public example and those who fail to repent 2:23.

In Luke 10:25–37, the parable of the Good Samaritan albeit an abstract character, illustrates what constitute neighborly and ethical behavior. The narrative explains while the Priest and Levite undoubtedly mitigated any moral responsibility and bypassed the wounded man, the Samaritan, however, took the initiative under universal moral obligation and tended to his needs; thus stripping away barriers, namely, race, ethnicity, religious traditions and creed. Groarke points out:

> The point of the imagined Good Samaritan episode is that *everybody* who needs our help is our neighbor. We are supposed to move beyond family members, beyond next-door neighbors, beyond fellow citizens, and beyond those who share the same religion, to embrace as a "neighbor" anyone in need. Jesus is, in effect, identifying a new "natural kind"—a moral natural kind—that is to authoritatively guide our behavior. He supplies a definition that identifies the essence of something—neighborliness—which is a traditional role for induction.[62]

Inductive cases usually require a pattern to exist between particular cases to make a viable inductive claim or generalization, but here Jesus draws "away a universal moral insight from one particular (imagined) incident."[63] This universal moral understanding that Jesus demonstrates is not bound to time constraints or cultural and ethnic sensitivity, but rather transcends them. The parable functions rhetorically since Jesus induces a response from the lawyer and forces him to reevaluate what neighborliness truly means.

---

61. 2 Kgs 9:30–37.
62. Groarke, "Jumping the Gaps," 497.
63. Groarke, "Jumping the Gaps," 497.

Induction and Example

The Analogy

Aristotle employs another type of reasoning; the analogy or argument from likeness, where the rhetor argues on the basis of similarity. This form of reasoning is analogous to the historical paradeigma because both reason by similarity. The analogy, however, is distinct in the sense the stratagem has a horizontal movement from one particular to another particular without necessarily expressing a universal.[64] Aristotle analogical reasoning explained:

> Further, you should carry on your questioning by means of similarity; for this is a plausible method, and the universal less obvious. For example, you should argue that, as knowledge and ignorance of contraries is the same thing, so is the perception of contraries the same thing, or, conversely, since the perception of them is the same, so also is the knowledge. This method resembles induction but is not the same thing; for, in induction, the universal is established from the particulars, whereas, in dealing with similars, what is established is not the universal under which all the similars fall.[65]

Paul Bartha states, "This passage occurs in a work that offers advice for framing dialectical arguments when confronting a somewhat skeptical interlocutor. In such situations, it is best not to make one's argument depend upon securing agreement about any universal proposition."[66] Groarke adds that the "analogy, like inductive syllogism, require some sort of penetrating gaze, a moment of immediate significance. One sees, one notices, one picks up on some significant similarity."[67] What one sees in A, one also sees in B, or what one observes in the previous case one also observes in the present case. The rhetorical objective of the author is not simply to amplify the similarities, but his greater ambition is to persuade the

---

64. I have stated Aristotle's historical examples expresses universals, this is not necessarily true for all historical examples in the NT. See Galatians, where Paul employs a universal for the "truth of the gospel."
65. Aristotle, *Top.* 8.1.
66. Bartha, "Analogy and Analogical Reasoning."
67. Groarke, *Aristotelian Account of Induction*, 216.

Identifying Biblical Example

auditors or readers to a draw a conclusion; not just any conclusion, but the conclusion he would have them draw.

The analogy is similarly expressed in the NT where biblical authors frequently use analogies to stress theological, eschatological, Jewish traditions, parables, ethics, social issues, or political matters to draw out the similarities. Two distinctive characteristics exist concerning the analogy and both are in concert with one another. First, the analogy is employed as a persuasive devise for the audience to accept a particular position, in which a conclusion is warranted. Second, an inference is made from the known quality of the primary analogy to the unknown quality of the secondary analogy. These analogies are often conjoined: (1) the historical and the present, and (2) the historical to the future.

The historical and the present analogy. In 1 Cor 10:1–13, Paul reinterprets this historical example when the Israelites ate spiritual food and drank from the rock in the wilderness, and the idolatry practices they committed.[68] He employs these dramatic events not to focus on Christ as the spiritual rock, which only have an ancillary meaning, but to point to the factualism that exist in the Corinthian church (secondary analogate) similar to the factions that existed in the exodus wilderness experience (primary analogate). Mitchell explains this succinctly:

> In 10:1–13 Paul presents an allegory to the factional strife which has succeeded the founding of the church at Corinth by appropriately choosing several events from Israel's wilderness wanderings which demonstrate the chosen people's destructive divisiveness after its "baptismal" exodus event.... There is thus a strong connection between the σχίσματα in the church community at Corinth and the scriptural allegories Paul employs in 1 Cor 10:1–13. It is clear from Philo and Josephus (and later rabbinic tradition) that all of the events in Israel's history which Paul draws on in 1 Cor 10:1–13 were regarded as examples of Factionalism at the time of Paul,

---

68. Nothing in the historical example suggests a generalization or universal is present.

Induction and Example

and were thus perfectly appropriate to the divisive situation which he faced at Corinth.[69]

In order for the analogy to be effective the new narrative must possess the same quality as the old one thus fulfilling the nature of the comparison. Albeit the old and new narrative have comparable analogies that one can garner, such as, they drank from the spiritual rock and Christ as the spiritual rock, the main judgment, however, behind the analogy is factionalism which Paul mainly sought after. He documents the Israelites past experience in the wilderness which he concludes, "These things happened to them as examples and were written down as warnings for us, on whom the culmination of the ages has come (1 Cor 10:11)." Thus, Paul's discovers an example from the past, to teach the Corinthian church to learn from the factious behavior of the Israelites, and that "God will bring destruction as God did to the wilderness generation if this disobedience continues, and all will be harmed."[70] What is true of the past, Israelites (A) will also be true of the future, the Corinthians (B) unless they change their factious behavior.

The historical to the future. The author employs a historical example to forecast events in the future. Aristotle reminds us that "no one can narrate things to come, but if there is narrative, it will be of things past, in order that, being reminded of them, the hearers may take better counsel about the future."[71] In Revelation, John is not necessarily guided in each and every instance by the spirit of prophecy uttering things that will come to pass, he simply attempts to explain "that God was indeed able to work great and wondrous plagues upon Egypt (and chose to act in this colorful manner, punishing by degrees and by diverse phenomena) so as to bring justice and deliverance to God's people—this fact lends plausibility to John's narration of a future in which God does this again. . . . John also capitalize on the tendency within scripture and within Jewish culture to portray God's future intervention in terms of God's prior

---

69. Mitchell, *Paul and the Rhetoric of Reconciliation*, 138–40.
70. Mitchell, *Paul and the Rhetoric of Reconciliation*, 253.
71. Aristotle, *Rhet.* 3.16.

Identifying Biblical Example

ones . . . [and] that people were willing to embrace a vision of the future more readily when it resembles the past."[72] One must bear in mind that John's rhetoric would lose its effectiveness if his audience did not perceive the potentiality or actuality for cosmological and ecocatastrophes were possible in the future.[73] The prophet's rhetoric is only as persuasive as the type of proofs employed (the result of the Egyptian plagues) and the means by which these proofs communicate the truth of his message. His message may run along these lines, if God, who intervened in the past and brought destructive plagues on Egypt (primary analogate), surely God is able to bring to fruition ecocatastrophe in the future (secondary analogate).

We see in chapter 9, the plague examples were designed to produce repentance, in which the prophet paints such a horrific scene that would scare a dead man, and although the plagues left destruction in its path killing a third of mankind, one would think those who survived and escaped the onslaught of devastation would take the opportunity to repent and refuse to worship things made with hands, but the text informs us, they remained unfazed and unwilling to repent.

Summary

The example is not an independent text and does not function in isolation from other texts, but rather is used as supporting main topics and subtopics. In order to aid the reader in identifying biblical example, the phrase "for example" often has to be applied in the text. What is more is that all historical paradeigmata employed in the NT are rhetorical, thus when an author recounts a past event the primary reason is to evoke a response by the current audience in the future. The biblical authors do not just repeat history, but are creative in their illustrations to address (i.e., church issues, theological, ethical, eschatological) the church in an entirely new setting.

72. DeSilva, *Seeing Things John's Way*, 308.
73. Johnson, "Earth's Ethos, Logos, and Pathos," 121. For sure, John's audience could probably sniff out the empty rhetoric of events that had no possibility of coming to pass.

5

Galatians

Arguing the Causa/Stasis

WHAT CAUSED THE CONFLICT in Galatia? The most likely historical scenario, as Paul constructs the situation, is that after Paul's initial visit to the churches in Galatia, Jewish Christian missionaries either from Antioch or Jerusalem came preaching another gospel that apparently insisted circumcision and certain facets of the Torah were a prerequisite to obtaining salvation in Christ. As Louis Martyn describes, these agitators, as they are familiarly called, interpreted "God's Christ in light of God's Law, rather than the Law in the light of Christ. This means that, in their Christology, Christ is secondary to the Law."[1] This is the complete opposite of the theology that Paul proclaimed.

There is reason to believe the agitators convincingly proclaimed a theology that was grounded in Scripture and so caused the Galatian churches to respond so quickly to their message (Gal 1:6), which is implied in the present tense, the verb μετατίθεσθε, "to change," indicates that the Galatians were changing, or were on the verge of changing their beliefs. Clinton Arnold contends, "The [agitators'] teaching would have resonated with the experience

---

1. Martyn, "Law-Observant Mission to Gentiles," 316.

the Galatians had with the gods in their pre-Christian practice. Performing the proper rites, not neglecting religious obligations, keeping the appointed festival times, keeping one's vows and maintain ritual purity were all vital to keep from the judgment of the gods."[2] Instead of remaining true to Paul's circumcision-free gospel for Gentiles, the Gentile Galatians inevitably decide that their best course of action was to return to paganism Gal 1:6–9; 4:8–11.[3] Clearly Paul saw this desertion and behavior as a real threat to the community well-being and thought a simple reassurance or reprimand would have been insufficient.[4] Thus his argument indicates that he had to tackle the issue head on by writing a letter rejecting the "different gospel" as truth-less.[5] Paul's rejection of the contrary gospel is confirmed by the Greek word θαυμάζω, "I marvel," Gal 1:6, also established specifically in Gal 3:1–5; 4:8–11; 5:7–10.[6]

Troy Martin employs the stasis theory approach in analyzing Paul's letter to the Galatians. He states that "stasis theory furnishes a means for moving from Paul's accusations and arguments to his understanding of the basic issue of the dispute."[7] In his analysis of Galatians, he identifies two accusations, one in Gal 1:6–9 and the other in Gal 4:8–11 that generate secondary and primary stases.[8] Thus Paul encountered two problems in Galatians, a gospel (or non-gospel) that requires circumcision and the other apostasy to paganism. The issue therefore in Galatians is not framed around the interrogative of Paul's apostolic authority. Johan Vos argues that "nowhere in the letter to the Galatians did Paul explicitly

2. He also concludes that "their insistence that the Galatians must be circumcised would have been a discouraging blow to them after the freedom of the Pauline gospel from such ritual obligations. Nevertheless, it would have made sense to them because the similarity to the structure of their former belief." Arnold, "I Am Astonished," 438–39.

3. Martin, "Apostasy to Paganism," 441.
4. Elmer, "Setting the Record Straight," 25.
5. Elmer, "Setting the Record Straight," 25.
6. Vos, "Paul's Argumentation in Galatians," 5–6.
7. Martin, "Apostasy to Paganism," 437.
8. Martin, "Apostasy to Paganism," 442. I will focus mainly on the secondary stasis generated by the accusation identified in Gal 1:6–9.

Induction and Example

present the legitimacy of his apostolate as the controversial point."[9] One particular example, Paul's convocation with the pillars of the church had more to do with defending the "truth of the gospel" than it did his apostleship 2:1–10.[10] If Paul was truly concerned that his authority was in serious jeopardy, his message would be different than what he currently wrote, and he would be attacking his opponents and defending himself instead.[11]

Nor is the dispute in Galatians between Paul and the agitators, but rather the different versions of the gospel they proclaim.[12] The agitators argued that their version of Torah law (and circumcision) for Gentile believers is true, and Paul counterargues or attempts to persuade the Galatians that his version of the gospel (circumcision free) is true; both are competing for the allegiance of the Galatians to adhere to their gospel (or non-gospel), this is one of the reasons the controversy exist, and without this contestation there would be no need for Paul to write Galatians.[13] Nowhere

---

9. Vos, "Paul's Argumentation in Galatians," 13. Bernard Lategan also notes that in "1:1–12 *apostolos* occurs only in 1:1, while all attention is focused on *euaggelion* as the main topic (1:6; 1:7 {2 xs}; 1:9 1:11 {2 xs}). In the letter as a whole, *apostolos* and its derivatives occur 4 times, *euaggelion* and its derivatives 14 times . . . the only reference is to him 'who called you. . . .'" Lategan, "Is Paul Defending His Apostleship," 417.

10. James D. Hester identifies the questioning of Paul's apostolic authority as the central issue. He argues the stasis is 1:11–12, and that Paul was accused of preaching an inferior gospel because he relied on, and sought out, instruction from the Jerusalem leaders. Hester, "Rhetorical Structure of Galatians," 227.

11. Witherington, *Grace in Galatia*, 30.

12. Justin K. Hardin believes that the letter is a contrast between Paul and the agitators. Hardin, "Galatians 1–2," 302–3.

13. Paul uses rhetoric to facilitate the discovery of the truth of the gospel through examples. Aristotle informs us that Rhetoric is "defined as the faculty of discovering the possible means of persuasion in reference to any subject whatever." Aristotle, *Rhet.* 1.1.2. In addition, although the letter is measured as Paul's pastoral response to the events that developed in Galatia, it is equally a rhetorical and exhortation letter intended to persuade because he had to diligently win back the Galatians' devotion to Christ and himself through the method of rhetoric; no other Pauline letter speaks to this truth. The other epistles that are rhetorical—e.g., Romans, 1–2 Corinthians, Philippians, and 1 Thessalonians do not deal with issues of apostasy and abandoning Christ.

in Paul's examples in the autobiographical section are the agitators addressed or referred to, nor are the examples meant to persuade them, the examples are meant to persuade the Galatians of the truth of the gospel. Although Paul critiques and condemns their behavior in chapters 3-6, this condemnation is the direct result of the circumcision gospel they proclaim.

Analysis of Paul's Sub-Issues

Most scholars agree that the *causa* is contained in Gal 1:6-9 (what brought the dispute into existence), but disagreements proliferate as to the syntax and import of vv. 10-12. The contention concerns whether to regard these verses as emanating from the *causa* vv. 6-9 or as ancillary issues, and how vv. 10-12 function in the autobiographical section of chs. 1-2.

I contend the sub-issues vv. 10-12 are not divorced from the causa vv. 6-9, but are inherently married to the Galatian controversy.[14] The gospel which Paul proclaims in (vv. 6-9) is rhetorically linked to his divine calling in vv. 11-12. Debbie Hunn notes that "verses 13-16 correspond to vv. 10-12 in that Paul first describes his past in vv. 13-14 (cp. v. 10) and then his commission to preach in vv. 15-16 (cp. vv. 11-12). Thus Paul links his former practice of pleasing people in v. 10 with his advancement in Judaism in vv. 13-14 to show that for him pleasing people has the goal of self-promotion.... Verses 13-24 therefore establish v. 10 that Paul no longer seeks to please people but God, and v. 10 gives the grounds for . . . 11-12 that his gospel is from God."[15] I would add, however, that vv. 21-24 does not attest to the people-pleasing contrast, rather, the pericope focuses mainly on Paul's independence and the testimony of the churches in Judea.

---

14. Martin correctly states that "God gave him this gospel through revelation (1:12), and Paul narrates his call to demonstrate that he does not persuade God (1:13-17). Since God entrusted him with this gospel (1:15-16), it is absurd to think that Paul now must persuade God of its validity." Martin, "Apostasy to Paganism," 447.

15. Hunn, "Pleasing God or Pleasing People?," 36.

Induction and Example

In Gal 1:13-16, Paul certainly contrasts pleasing people with pleasing God, and he contrasts his own past actions vv. 13-14 with his present actions vv. 15-16. The other instances where the pleasing people or pleasing God syncrisis is demonstrated are the meeting with the church pillars in Jerusalem and the Antiochian event Gal 2:1-14. Brian Dodd makes the point, "This self characterisation in 1:10 anticipates his confrontation of his Jerusalem opponents in 2.4-5. The remembrance of them serves as an opportunity for Paul to demonstrate how he is Christ's bondservant, and not a people pleaser."[16] The antithesis in Antioch is between Peter who is deemed to be seeking the favor of men because he assented to the theology of the circumcision group, and Paul, who remained steadfast as a servant of Christ when he spoke against Peter's behavior Gal 2:11-14.

An Analysis and Function of Paul's Examples in Gal 1-2

We have discussed the *casua* and the stasis as it pertains to what brought the dispute into existence, as well as other sub-issues. The next point of contention in scholarly debates is determining how Paul uses examples, which scholars have theorized endlessly about the purpose of his self-reference motifs. Some conclude that he is responding to accusations levied against the legitimacy of his apostleship and therefore uses personal examples to defend his case. Others argue that Paul espouses the nature and origins of his gospel and therefore argues on that basis.[17] George Lyons and Beverly Gaventa present another popular theory by arguing that Paul's narrative remarks elevating himself are archetypical of how the gospel works as a paradigm.[18]

To the first interpretive point, I have already discussed it was not Paul's primary intent to argue for the legitimacy of his

---

16. Dodd, "Christ's Slave," 100.
17. Vos, "Paul's Argumentation in Galatians," 14.
18. Gaventa, "Galatians 1 and 2," 326.

apostleship. To the second point, I agree, as most scholars do, that Paul is trying to demonstrate the divine origins of his gospel and his independence from the other apostles. However, I take issue with the last point. In her article, Hunn questions the legitimacy of Lyons and Gaventa's paradigm view and concludes that "although Paul embodies upright behavior in Galatians 1–2 and ought to be used as a paradigm where possible—it is not the purpose of these two chapters to show this."[19] She explains further in some detail:

> According to the paradigm view, the power of the gospel wrought this change in Paul, and he encourages the Galatians to follow his example. Does this mean, then, that the gospel affected the other apostles in the same way? If so, it seems odd that in chap. 1 Paul avoids encountering them, men who were also changed by the power of the gospel. If not, it says little for Paul's point if the leaders of the movement were themselves unaffected by the power Paul argues it had. Paul's narrative in 2, 11–14 tells against the paradigm view as well. In Antioch, Peter still agreed with Paul about the gospel (2, 16). Paul, however, accused him of walking away from the truth of the gospel by refusing to eat any longer with the Gentiles (2, 14). In other words, Peter's departure from the gospel was behavioral, not doctrinal or intellectual—he still knew it was Christ who justifies, and who justifies without the law. But if Paul is attempting to show the power of the gospel to change character, he undermines his case when he includes the examples of Peter, Barnabas, and the Jewish Christians with them, whose belief in the gospel failed to produce appropriate behavioral changes in them. To strengthen that case, Paul should have omitted this section. In fact, the claim that Paul is proving the power of the gospel to change character, a fundamental claim of the paradigm view, is also a major weakness of the view.[20]

Along with Hunn, I contend that Paul's examples do not function morally but rhetorically. The only instance in the narratives where Paul demonstrates the effectiveness of the gospel upon one's life

19. Hunn, "Pleasing God or Pleasing People?," 31.
20. Hunn, "Pleasing God or Pleasing People?," 32.

Induction and Example

is his own Gal 1:13–16, 21–24; 2:19–20, and the paradigm view scarcely represents the overall narratives in chs. 3–6. Vos argues that those who favor this interpretation often cite Gal 4:12 as the main support for their analysis but then ignore that this verse belongs to an entirely different context.[21] The paradigm view quells the efficacy of Paul's examples, it is not how the gospel works that Paul gives emphasis to, but how his personal examples address the situation that arose in Galatia.

We should note that the examples Paul employs are stressed more than any other rhetorical technique thus giving insight into his strategy in arguing for the truth of the gospel. Aristotle makes the point that "rhetorical speeches are sometimes characterized by examples and sometimes by enthymemes, and orators themselves may be similarly distinguished by their fondness for one or the other."[22] Although Paul has a preference for example, the enthymeme is not absent in the autobiographical section Gal 1:13—2:14. Paul A. Holloway, for instance, identifies a complex enthymeme structure within the present example in Gal 2:14. He writes:

> Paul saw in this retraction a perversion of the gospel, and he confronted Peter with the following question: εἰ σὺ Ἰουδαῖος ὑπάρχων ἐθνικῶς καὶ οὐκ Ἰουδαϊκῶς ζῇς, πῶς τὰ ἔθνη ἀναγκάζεις ἰουδαΐζειν? In this complex enthymeme Paul alleges as many as three contradictions in Peter's behavior: first, he is compelling Gentiles to live as Jews (τὰ ἔθνη ἀναγκάζεις ἰουδαΐζειν); second, he is enforcing a standard from which he himself has just recently departed (σὺ ... οὐχὶ Ἰουδαϊκῶς ζῇς); and third, he has not held to this standard even though he is himself a Jew (Ἰουδαῖος ὑπάρχων).[23]

The enthymeme is assimilated within the example, but the overall scope and purpose of the example remains the principal part of his argument or proofs.[24]

---

21. Vos, "Paul's Argumentation in Galatians," 15.
22. Aristotle, *Rhet.* 1.2. 10–11.
23. Holloway, "Enthymeme," 335–36.
24. Although scholars recognize enthymemes in the text, it is unlikely the

Galatians

There are several reasons why Paul may have employed the examples. The first reason. It is likely that Paul deliberately uses the examples because they are practical and lucid in nature and thus gives a clearer picture, enabling the Galatians to comprehend the similarities between his past experiences involving the truth of the gospel and their present understanding of it. The past examples explain the present and the present points to the future.[25] Aristotle forms a rhetorical question:

> Why do people enjoy paradigms and stories more than enthymemes in rhetorical speeches? Is it because they enjoy learning, and quickly? But they learn more easily by paradigms and stories; for what they come to know are these particular things, but enthymemes are demonstration from universals, which we know less than particulars. Further, we are more inclined to believe what many bear witness to, and paradigms and stories are more like witnesses; and the proofs that come from witnesses are easy (to obtain).[26]

Unlike deductive arguments or the enthymeme which require the auditors or readers to possess more skill and understanding the rigors of this form of reasoning, the inductive example require less skill and not as rigorous to comprehend by the general assembly or the common person. The Galatians would have been able to identify with Paul's simplistic examples and make the necessary connection that the truth of the gospel is at the heart of the examples. Admitting that the examples Paul employs are simplistic in nature, one must not overlook or minimize the rhetorical skill Paul possessed to cognitively search his diverse and expansive (albeit early) ministry to discover the right type of example that fall within the same class of the Galatians' controversy. Thus, his previous experience became the primary nexus that brought awareness and universal knowledge to a new particular situation; not any preexisting names, topics or events, but his own personal experience. He

---

Galatians would have had the skills to discern the enthymemes.
25. Gerhardsson, *Memory and Manuscript*, xi.
26. Aristotle, *Probl.* 18.3.

Induction and Example

created and coined his own special topic; the phrase "the truth of the gospel" to address the Galatians' dispute.[27]

The second reason. Examples are not like leaves that fall aimlessly into a speech without purpose.[28] They find their way into the text by the author. These series of examples that Paul employs in chapters 1–2 do not stand alone or occur in a vacuum Gal 1:21–24, 2:1–10, 2:11–14, he uses them to argue the *causa* Gal 1:6–9 and sub-issues Gal 1:10–12. Aristotle states, "If we have no enthymemes, we must employ examples as demonstrative proofs, for conviction is produced by these; but if we have them, examples must be used as evidence and as a kind of epilogue to the enthymemes ... if they [examples] stand last they resemble evidence, and a witness is in every case likely to induce belief."[29] To Aristotle's latter point, if the enthymeme precedes the example, the example(s) should be used as a type of epilogue or substantiation to the enthymeme. Vos identifies the following syllogism in the *causa*:

> 1a. The gospel is true if it is proclaimed by a true servant of God and Christ.
>
> 1b. The gospel is false if it is proclaimed by a flatterer and a servant of humans.
>
> 2. The content and the tone of Gal 1:6–9 demonstrate that I am not a flatterer and a servant of humans but a true servant of God and Christ.
>
> 3. Consequently, the gospel I proclaimed to you is true.[30]

It merits attention these examples that Paul employs to argue the *causa* are not the reason why he wrote Galatians. The examples that he constructs of himself are external and originally had nothing to do with the crisis that took place in Galatia, and yet these proofs which are inductive in nature are analogous to rather than the opposite of the events that arose in Galatia.

---

27. Ebeling, *Truth of the Gospel*, vii.
28. Gelley, *Unruly Examples*, 1.
29. Aristotle, *Rhet.* 2.20.
30. Vos, "Paul's Argumentation in Galatians," 10.

Galatians

On this account, Paul shapes each example without interruption around the Galatian controversy. We can divide Gal 1:13—2:14 as such: 1:13-16 is a contrast (Paul as a persecutor of the church / Paul as proclaimer of the gospel), 1:17-20 is informational materiel, and 1:21-24; 2:1-10; 2:11-14 are examples. It is important to bear in mind that by removing the contrast, and the three examples that follow, would essentially remove Paul's supporting evidence for the truth of the gospel; the majority or almost all of the first two chapters of his autobiographical section. Outside the causa and subtopics 1:6-9, 10-12, he does not address the Galatians about the specifics of the accusation until 3:1-5. After expounding on the Antiochian example 2:15-20, the next example begins at 3:6-9.

This brings us to the last reason. The use of a historical or present example requires a judgment to be made from the audience about their future, it is not merely used to occupy space in a speech or letter, but the proof always has a rhetorical purpose. To be effective, and have the prospect to persuade, the example or examples must be contextualized in such a way that address the audience current situation. As Lyons explains, "examples, in short, do not happen; they are made."[31] As we have it, all of Paul's examples are in, and now the Galatians are required to deliberate as readers and hearers, and make a community judgment based on Paul's usage of his personal examples. This consequential decision is not predicated forensically on their past actions or behavior, or Paul's apostleship which is negligible, rather, the community must actively participate, interpret, and determine how to proceed in regard to their own future.[32] To be sure, the Galatians would also consider the agitators' various arguments and proofs, and since they were on the verge of turning from Paul's gospel, to the agitators' persuasive non-gospel, Paul must prove through his examples that his gospel is true.

---

31. Lyons, *Exemplum*, 33.

32. Dodd contends that just as Paul rejected those who opposed the truth of the gospel in Jerusalem and Antioch, he exhorts the Galatians to demonstrate the same boldness against the agitators. Dodd, "Christ's Slave," 100-102.

Induction and Example

Nevertheless, the acceptance or rejection of Paul's examples (that his gospel originated with God, and verified by the Judean churches and the apostles in Jerusalem) will determine whether they will remain free in Christ or be in bondage to the law, and coupled with to be free from, or enslaved to, the "miserable principles" of the world. Since Paul's examples are structured and based on the truth of the gospel, he is optimistic that truth will prevail. Aristotle informs us that "the true and the just are naturally superior to their opposites, so that, if decisions are improperly made, they must owe their defeat to their own advocates; which is reprehensible."[33] Thus, Paul was confident whether through the Lord, his pastoral care or his rhetorical ability, they would rethink their position by reflecting on the examples and their communal experiences with him, and return to Christ and himself Gal 4:12–20; 5:10.

Paul's Inductive Experience and Paul's Inductive Theology

Almost all scholars recognize that after Paul's encounter with Christ his person radically changed from one who repudiated those devoted to the living Christ Gal 1:13–14, to one who now bears the marks of Christ on his body Gal 6:17. Paul articulates his transformative experience in Christ, by stating, "I have been crucified with Christ and I no longer live, but Christ lives in me. The life I now live in the body, I live by faith in the Son of God, who loved me and gave himself for me Gal. 2:20." He distinguishes the old self that died to sin from the new one, this new life that he now leads in Christ is only made possible through the Damascus experience; not by the law but living out that reality through faith in Christ.

As a result of the manifestation of Christ in Paul's life, his hermeneutics on the Hebrew and Septuagint provides new meaning in a different, broader context. His theology of Christ is also reshaped before there was Mosaic law, but now Paul argues there

---

33. Aristotle, *Rhet.* 1.1.12.

Galatians

is a law of Christ and a law of faith Rom 3:27; Gal 6:2.[34] Not only did Paul's experience of Christ transform his theology of the law, but his ideology on the eschaton altered the way he thinks eschatologically. Arland J. Hultgren states Paul was "the first major theologian in the history of Christianity to leave a literary legacy of his thinking that has remained for subsequent generations."[35] The universal church is therefore reliant on, and indebted to Paul, for understanding what it means to have a personal relationship with Christ, and surely his writing and the memory of the early stages of the ecclesia. One can imagine the scriptural and spiritual implication of the absence of Pauline theology and the vacancy of his letters (his biography sketched in Acts), and to understand what it means to be justified by faith without the works of the law, let alone other Pauline themes.

To unfold further both Paul's experience and theology, Aristotle explains the difference between those who only have experience and those who have the experience and the art. He states, "In general the sign of knowledge or ignorance is the ability to teach, and for this reason we hold that art rather than experience is scientific knowledge; for the artist can teach, but the others cannot."[36] Aristotle contends further "we must not ask every question of each individual expert, nor is the expert bound to answer everything that is asked of him about each given subject, but only such questions as fall within the scope of his own science."[37] Aristotle is not suggesting from a modern perspective that a gastrologist should

---

34. Tobin explains the believer "by being guided by the Spirit and loving one another through the practice of virtue, are equivalently carrying out what had been central to the Mosaic Law. They are fulfilling the law, but they are not, as such observing it." Tobin, *Paul's Rhetoric in Its Context*, 69–70.

35. Hultgren, "Paul as Theologian," 359.

36. Aristotle, *Metaph.* 981b 12. It is important to note, in Aristotle's *Metaphysics*, he provides his two level theory of knowledge. In *Nicomachean Ethics*, however, he presents a three-level theory of the theoretical (*episteme*), which can explain why something is; the technical or artistic (*techne*), which can explain how to do something; and the practical (*phronesis*), which explains how to live. Experience provides the material cause for all of these types of knowledge.

37. Aristotle, *An. post.* 1.12.

Induction and Example

have the expertise of a cardiologist because this is outside his or her own science and specification, what he requires of the gastrologist is to have more than general knowledge in that particular domain, and to have the ability to explain the reason, and the science behind gastroenterology.[38]

Taking into account Aristotle's philosophy and what constitutes the ability to teach, and apply it to Paul, his experience alone does not necessarily qualify him to teach. What makes Paul a first rate theologian is his intimate personal experience of Christ, along with his ability to explain the reasons behind what he knows enables him to teach. Not the things outside the theologies and domain of God, rather his ability to teach and explain spiritual things about God in Christ and the church.[39] He certainly had the authority to speak on and solve doctrinal issues within the church.[40] The reader should remember that Paul was a Pharisaic academic, a trained exegete in the law and Hebrew scripture, which enables him to speak dogma (Acts 22:3).

If we ask Paul the nature of God's grace, he can say, I experienced it firsthand, and therefore I can explain it. God's grace

---

38. See appendix on experience and universal.

39. Obviously Paul does not have scientific knowledge such as the ability to explain how the earth rotates around the sun. Moreover, I am not suggesting that Paul is in full possession of knowledge about God, but rather he is in the position to teach spiritual things as they relate to Christ. He certainly thought he was in possession of the truth of the gospel. I must add also, unquestionably scholars and theologians have made enormous contributions in their writing on the biblical text, and can teach the Bible with skill (those who may not know God on a personal level). My point here is that Paul had the experience of Christ, and the Hebraic training, to write about him on both levels. If Paul did not have the experience of Christ, he would not have been able to write the things which he did. And thus so many elements of his experience with Christ would be missing in Pauline literature such as, "in Christ," "with Christ," "Christ lives in me," I am "crucified with Christ," "if anyone is in Christ, he is a new creation," etc. These experiences shaped his theology.

40. Gerhardsson, *Memory and Manuscript*, 303. In 1 Thess 4:15, Paul reassures the Thessalonians about the resurrection of Christ. In Gal 1:7–8, Paul has the authority to pronounce a curse. In Romans, Paul explains the concept, behavior, and consequence of sin. In 1 Cor 4:1, Paul declares he was entrusted as a steward of the mysteries of God.

Galatians

reached me on the Damascus road, and if it can reach me, it can reach anyone, the worst of sinners, the one who persecuted the church of Christ 1 Tim 1:15–16. It should be observed, however, that Paul did not chronicle his religious experiences simply to explain what God did for, and through him, rather, he always interpreted his own experience in view of others.[41] Thus, he understood the theology of grace, and that God's grace is not restricted to time and space, or race, but is universally available to all humanity, Rom 5:20; 6:14; Gal 1:15, 2:21; 2 Cor 1–10.[42]

If Paul claimed we are sinners without explaining the cause, it would certainly bring the theology of sin in question and the genesis of it. He therefore supplies the underlying causes on certain topics such as the nature, work, and consequence of sin, because he is a hamartiologist.[43] No other epistle captures the influx of his ideology and notion of sin more than the epistle to the Romans. Let us analyze a particular passage in Romans inductively. First, to assist in this analysis, Groarke explains, Aristotle's induction "depends crucially on a relationship of identity or resemblance, the number of specimens examined is not a central issue. If we have identical objects A and B, then what is true of A must be true of B. When we have examined A, we have no need to examine B."[44] In Rom 5:12, Paul does not enumerate or need to analyze every person behavior (on planet earth) to determine that people possess the same sinful nature of Adam (he can look at himself and examine his own actions to determine that), and that we all die in Adam. He makes the inductive connection, and understands the one affects the all, thus exhibiting the principles of induction. Paul's induction can be stated: what is true of A (Adam) is also true of B (humans). It satisfies the law of resemblance, all humans possess humanness. Thus a

---

41. Engberg-Pedersen, "Construction of Religious Experience," 150.

42. Fee, *1 and 2 Timothy, Titus*, 54. See also 2 Cor 12:9; 1 Cor 15:10.

43. See Dunn, *Theology of Paul*, for an explanation of the so called "original sin" and the different views of Adam in noncanonical literature before and after Paul (79–101). Even if, perhaps, the concept of death and sin did not originate with Paul, he viewed and interpreted these preexistent theologies differently.

44. Groarke, *Aristotelian Account of Induction*, 136–37.

Induction and Example

universal relationship and the capacity to sin exist for all humans. Paul demonstrates his theology through an inductive syllogism:

> 1. Particular case: Just as sin came into the world through one man, and death through sin,
>
> 2. Universal—and so death spread to all men, because all sinned,
>
> 3. Thus—death spread to all because of one man's sin (see also Rom 5:13–20; chs. 6–7).

In the highly discussed and debatable verses of Gal 2:15–21, Paul contrast between those who are justified by faith in Christ outside the observance of the law and those who depend on the law for justification. In 2:16, he states, "Know that a person is not justified by the works of the law, but by faith in Jesus Christ. So we, too, have put our faith in Christ Jesus that we may be justified by faith in Christ and not by the works of the law, because by the works of the law no one will be justified." In Paul's reasoning, he does not negotiate or variate his concept of justification, he does not give credence to some you are either justified or not. This point is very important, and Heikki Raisanen concludes:

> Jew as well as Gentiles must enter the new community. This necessarily implies that the old covenant no longer works . . . such a soteriological exclusivism reveals the degree of discontinuity between Judaism and Paul. Faith in Jesus involved quite a new step for a Jew. He had to enter the new community, socially distinct form the synagogue even when loyalty to the synagogue was maintained (own services, liturgy etc.).[45]

Paul contends that those who believe in Jesus are one in the family of God, and that there is no further need to be circumcised whether Jew or Greek. John W. Taylor asserts, "Paul places Jews and Gentiles on the same level: sinners in need of justification in Christ."[46] It does not work for Paul that Gentiles only need to be

---

45. Raisanen, "Galatians 2:16," 549.
46. Taylor, "Demonstrating Transgression," 549.

Galatians

justified before God, but rather he concludes Jews are also in need of justification. Clearly being justified by faith was consequential with Paul because he too personally recognized the need for it.

The Galatians' Inductive Experience

As the previous points have shown, Paul's inductive experience became the basis for understanding the reality of God in Christ. His experiences speak to his intimate and permanent and inseparable relationship with Christ that guides his ethical life, his theology, and eschatology. The complete opposite occurs, however, with the Galatians' inductive experience, their relationship with Christ prove not to be permanent but ephemeral. Paul declares they ran well for a moment (Gal 5:7), but their course of action changed, once the agitators arrived in Galatia proclaiming a persuasive message that hindered their progression (Gal 5:8).[47]

In Gal 3:1–5, Paul ushers in their personal experience of the Spirit and the miraculous deeds performed in their community to reason against them, and to persuade them, for the truth of the gospel. Thus Paul pulls up their past to guide their future response. James Dunn states whenever Paul has concerns with the commitment of the initial recipients of his gospel message, he always refers them back to their initial act of hearing and experience of grace.[48] The central point in Paul's argument is that he is critical of their capacity to comprehend the true nature of their experience.[49] Paul asks, "Are you so foolish" (3:3), or in Leon Morris's rendering, "Are you mindless?" Thus Paul openly expresses his discontent with

---

47. This hindrance of obeying the truth of the gospel was not self-inflicted or derived from their own reasoning, rather, the negative influence of the agitators. Morris, *Galatians*, 159.

48. Dunn, *Theology of Paul*, 324.

49. It is often debated whether *epathete* should be interpreted as "suffer" or "experience" (3:4). I agree with Matera, who contends the word is better translated as "experience" than "suffer" since the context is in reference to the Spirit. Matera, *Galatians*, 113.

Induction and Example

the Galatians for their lack of spiritual acumen in being so easily duped and swayed by the agitators.

The initial reception of the Spirit, and the continuation of the manifestation of the Spirit, and the miracles performed in their community speak to their new reality and existence in Christ (Gal 3:2–5). In addition, the crying of "Abba Father" in their hearts is also a potent sign they are sons of God (4:1–7). These memory-facts of various kinds were planted in their souls and created powerful experiences and generated cumulative knowledge. They experienced God on such a profound level with undeniable evidence, this should have grounded their faith and secured their commitment and awareness about God's gracious activities, and the certainty of their position they already had in Christ.[50] But they astonishingly desire to abandon both Christ and the agitators, in favor of an old religious experience, namely, a return to paganism.[51] They had a past life in bondage, and a present life in freedom in Christ, and yet, desire to return to a future life in bondage.

Ironically, the Galatians desired to return to paganism or another course of worship; the Israelites also experienced God's various manifestations and provisions of manna and water in the wilderness for forty years, and yet, they still decided their best course of action was to turn to idolatry when Aaron, encouraged by the people, posed an alternative course of worship. History has a tendency to repeat itself when an individual or Christian communities are confronted with enticing religiosities and ideologies,

---

50. See appendix on memory and experience. Undoubtedly, these experiences were not one-time events nor did the experiences stop, but the Galatians continued to experience the Spirit and God's gracious activities.

51. This old religious experience should not be interpreted as a return to Judaism but a return to paganism. Martin states, ". . . as evidenced by their renewed observance of their former pagan time-keeping scheme" (4:10). Martin, *Apostasy to Paganism*, 449. Similarly, Polhill asserts, "Before Christ came to them they most likely had worshiped the religion of nature, like the cult of Cybele with its emphasis on the turning seasons. Bound to the fatalism of an endless cycle of seasons and to the fear of nature's forces, they were enslaved by their belief in powers which were in reality no gods at all. By submitting to the law they were falling back into the same kind of slavery-bound to rules, no longer free." Polhill, *Paul and His Letters*, 150.

and decide to abandon the certainty of their experiences (in God in Christ) that grounded their faith. These biblical narratives demonstrate that "similar results naturally arise from similar causes"; for the future every so often resembles the past.[52]

Nevertheless, Paul argues that the Galatians, ἐναρξάμενοι, "having started," in the Spirit, the greater, tried to be "perfected in the flesh," the lesser (v. 3). The Galatians thought or were persuaded to think by the agitators the gospel that Paul preached was a lesser form of the gospel, and to perfect their faith, they had to observe certain aspects of the law, and circumcision. In Paul's reasoning, however, this is inconsistent with the truth of gospel, in which no further steps were needed for the Galatians in becoming full members of the community of faith than the one they initially had, and that is having faith in the crucified Jesus. In the grand picture of things, Paul's logic indicates that if the Spirit is the sole reason for the Galatians' existence, and the Spirit continues to work in them, how can they be justified by the law 3:1–5? While Paul needs to remind the Galatians of their experience in Christ, his point is to show how their experience in him signifies their justification, and how they are now partakers in the blessing of Abraham.

This new experience in Christ initiated by the Spirit is the identity marker that proves they belong to Christ.[53] Stephen Fowl concludes that Paul sees the Galatians' experience of the Spirit of God and evaluate that experience as a sign of the blessing promised to Abraham.[54] Hunn equally states:

> The introduction of the Spirit is not a movement away from justification. Instead Paul ties it to the Galatians' experience of the Spirit by equating the justification of Gentiles with the blessing of Abraham in 3:8, and the blessing of Abraham with the sending of the Spirit in 3:14.23. . . . In 3:2 Paul begins to open the eyes of the Galatians to their experience of the Spirit. He does not ask, "How were you justified?" to people now uncertain

---

52. Aristotle, *Rhet.* 1.4.9.
53. Fee, *God's Empowering Presence*, 383. See also 1:6; 4:20.
54. Fowl, "Who Can Read Abraham's Story?," 83–84.

about how justification takes place. He asks instead how they received the Spirit because the miracles told them they had received the Spirit and because receiving the Spirit was proof of justification. Therefore, with the introduction of the Spirit in 3:2 Paul continues his theme from chapter 2, and this places both 2:16 and 3:2, 5 in the context of justification.[55]

Although the theme of justification that Paul started in 2:15 appears to be abandoned in favor of the Galatians' experience, in 3:1, Hunn has shown that justification is inherently intertwined with the Galatians' inductive experience.

Summary

I contend Paul's inductive experiences are not employed to defend his apostolic authority but rather to defend the truth of the gospel. These examples are artistic in nature, tailored, and applicable to the circumstances that took place in Galatia. I argue further that Paul's experiences shaped his theology of Christ and the way he interpret scripture. In addition, Paul is critical of the Galatians' lack of devotion to Christ and himself by being enthralled with the agitators' circumcision gospel. He contends the Galatians' inductive experience should have been proof that they already received Christ and the Spirit without the application of the law.

---

55. Hunn, "ΠΙΣΤΙΣ ΧΡΙΣΤΟΥ in Galatians 2:16," 31. Fee also explains that "the key element of Christian conversion is the Spirit, dynamically explained (3:2–5; 4:6) as the fulfillment of the promise to Abraham 3:14 . . . thus the Spirit not only stands at the beginning of Christian existence, but is the key ingredient to Paul's understanding of the whole of that existence." Fee, *God's Empowering Presence*, 370.

6

Paul's Inductive Examples

I DESCRIBED BEFOREHAND THAT Paul's inductive experience emerge through a particular event on the Damascus road which is his starting point with Christ, and that he experiences other particular events in Christ (revelation or visions, etc.) which guide his ethics and epistemology. He reflected and wrote on his experiences in which he induces certain truths about the nature of God/Christ which lead him to affirm, draw generalizations, and universal conclusions.

I explicate here that Paul sets out to prove and to persuade the Galatians that his gospel is true and has divine origins, and the agitators' gospel is false, from four paradeigmata: The Judean churches (1:21–24), Jerusalem (2:1–10), Antioch (2:11–14), and Abraham's inductive experience (3:6–9). These examples substantiate his present proposition for the "truth of the gospel" (Gal 1:6–9, 10–12). In *On the Freedom of the Rhodians* the author writes:

> To prove the truth of the argument that people are always accorded their rights in proportion to their ability to assert them, Demosthenes adduces the example of the two treaties that the Hellenes have with the Great King (an example "known to you all"): one, made by

Induction and Example

the Athenians, which is praised by all; the other, made by the Lacedaemonians, which all condemn. Though neither treaty is named, it would seem reasonable to assume that the former is the Peace of Callias, the latter that of Antalcides.[1]

The rhetoric behind the treaty is to adduce examples to establish a proposition (to prove the truth of the argument that people are always accorded their rights in proportion to their ability to assert them). These examples are not ambiguous nor foreign to the hearers; they are binary to proliferate persuasion and manipulate the audience decision in the future. Benoit makes the point: "The greater number of examples adduced by the speaker, the more persuasive the argument by example will be. This is a reasonable notion for confidence in the truth of the generalizations—and therefore in the conclusion—is likely to increase as the number of instances supporting it increases."[2] In our case, Paul ushers in multiple examples not without reason, they are employed deliberately to enhance credibility more cogently that his theology of Christ and his circumcision free-gospel is true. If Paul employed one example instead of four, it would certainly lessen the conviction and representation of them being true.

These examples that Paul employs have a movement from part to whole to part with the explicit use of a universal proposition. To prove his case in the present (the Galatians' controversy-part), Paul discloses similar inductive experiences from his past and Abraham's inductive experience (examples-whole) that are in the same class or genus with the truth of the gospel in Galatia. He rhetorically applies these examples which forms the universal principle, to another particular or to the conclusion the Galatians must induce from them (to reject the agitators' gospel and remain free in Christ-part). Thus the examples Paul constructs are meant to persuade, but also to promote one universal (principle) proposition: the truth of the gospel. Lyons explains with "the multiplicity of example: many historical events mentioned together invite the

---

1. Milns, *Historical Paradigms*, 25.
2. Benoit, *Aristotle's Example*, 191.

reader to relate them to a general rule."³ The truth of the gospel for Paul is a timeless principle that judges the quality of the gospel in any generation.

To augment, and authenticate the veracity of his universal principle of the "truth of the gospel," Paul cuts no corners and equally pronounces a universal curse on anyone including himself, and angels, who proclaims a different gospel than the one he proclaimed (Gal 1:8-9). Tolmie explains that Paul "conveys the message that the gospel is more important than any human being—even himself. It has its own existence and independence," because "it is based on divine authority."⁴ In this regard, the agitators are subject to the curse because they proclaim a gospel that require Gentles to be circumcised.

In addition, these examples are in concert with the overall theme of liberty exhibited throughout the letter and communicated in the conclusion. Paul concludes, "It is for freedom that Christ has set us free. Stand firm, then, and do not let yourselves be burdened again by a yoke of slavery. Mark my words! I, Paul, tell you that if you let yourselves be circumcised, Christ will be of no value to you at all Gal 5:1-2." Rudolph H. Blank asserts:

> While Paul in Galatians speaks of freedom and liberty primarily in terms of freedom from circumcision and from the impositions of Mosaic Law, the concept of freedom in Galatians and the rest of Paul's epistles is much wider than just freedom from the Law. The freedom of those who belong to God's new people includes freedom from occult powers. This is especially the case of those Gentile members of the Galatian congregations who formerly worshipped idols and were involved in all manner of occult activity.⁵

This freedom from occultic powers is associated with having faith in Christ, and in him they must remain. The Galatians must also reject the proposition that to be full members of the new

3. Lyons, *Exemplum*, 26.
4. Tolmie, *Rhetorical Analysis*, 49.
5. Blank, *Six Theses concerning Freedom in Christ*, 250.

Induction and Example

community they must embrace the law and be circumcised (as a form of justification).⁶

Example One: The Testimony of the Judean Churches (Gal 1:21–24)

> Then I went to Syria and Cilicia. I was personally unknown to the churches of Judea that are in Christ. They only heard the report: "The man who formerly persecuted us is now preaching the faith he once tried to destroy." And they praised God because of me.

In this pericope, Paul begins by employing the adverb ἔπειτα, "then," the second of three he uses in the autobiographical section. The second ἔπειτα is consistent with the first one depicting the chronological order of his activities, but this ἔπειτα also introduces Paul's inartificial proof, namely, the testimony of the churches. This authoritative witness exist outside the Galatian controversy, in which Paul uses artistically as an example to validate the nature of his gospel.⁷ This example like the following paradeigmata are used solely on the grounds to argue his causa or what caused the conflict in Galatia (1:6–9).

This concise narrative does not receive enough attention from scholars, one reason is probably due to its nature and brevity; the other perhaps due to the absence of any confrontational motifs that Paul had with others in subsequent narratives (Gal 2:1–14). Despite the lack of dissension the narrative is not without purpose; for almost all scholars are inclined to associate Paul's travels with his independence from the Jerusalem apostles. Martinus C. de Boer explains Paul's independent gospel:

---

6. Loubser, "Contrast Slavery/Freedom," 172.
7. Aristotle states that "although the use of inartificial proofs is almost entirely confined to forensic oratory, they *may* be used in deliberative oratory." Aristotle, *Rhet.* 1.15.3, note a.

Paul's Inductive Examples

After passing through the province of Judea on his way to Syria and Cilicia after his first visit to Jerusalem. Paul was from then on and for more than a decade personally unknown to the Jewish Christian churches in Judea, including the one in Jerusalem. He could not therefore have been an apostle of these churches, charged with preaching a version of the gospel approved by the Jerusalem apostles, one that he allegedly distorted when he went to Gentile territory. He has always been the apostle of Christ to the Gentiles, preaching the gospel that he also preached to the Galatians, from the moment of his conversion and call.[8]

I agree, as most scholars do, that Paul avers the divine origin of his gospel, because he seeks to stress his independence from the other apostles in Gal 1:1, 11–12. It should be noted, Paul's primary concern was not to demonstrate his evangelistic activities; he only remarks of these geographic areas because they were assimilated in his rhetorical proof. The responsibility of a skilled rhetor was to compose a speech using applicable material that advances his argument, and casting aside all material that are of no consequence. If Paul was truly absorbed in naming the whereabouts of his missionary activities and the experiential details undoubtedly he would have.

On the basis thereof, Paul conveniently detours this irrelevant material and concentrates on external proofs that are of greater import. He mentions his former life as a persecutor of the church because the nature of his persecution which only procures meaning

---

8. De Boer, *Galatians*, 101. D. Verseput explains that "by asserting his independence from the Jerusalem apostles and the Jewish mission in general, Paul is affirming the independence of Gentile salvation from the Torah covenant." Verseput, "Paul's Gentile Mission," 43. N. H. Taylor asserts, "It is only if he can demonstrate that his authority pertained prior to his association with other Christian leaders that Paul can claim that it is unaffected by the state of his relations with those leaders. By identifying his vocation as he presently understood and exercised it as the purpose of his conversion, Paul implies that this vocation antecedes his acquaintance with Peter and membership of the Antiochene church. It is this claim that Paul seeks to demonstrate in relating key episodes and developments in his subsequent career in the following verses." Taylor, "Paul's Apostolic Legitimacy," 71.

Induction and Example

in collaboration with the churches testimony and the faith he now proclaims. The Judean churches heard that Paul no longer persecuted those of "the faith" but equally preaches the same "faith" as they had.[9] Thus, it is not insignificant that Paul makes known that his faith is congruent with the churches who preached it earlier.

Paul's Rhetorical Agenda

As previously noted, Paul's letter is designed for persuasion, and his rhetorical aptitude is probably more on full display than the ensuing examples 2:1–14; 3:1–5. He includes the responses of the Judean churches as verification claims, as proofs. As an incisive rhetor, Paul does not testify or vaunt his gospel is divine and ordained by God, instead he relies on the opinions of the orthodox churches for this verbal commitment. Aristotle mentions that the orator should seek after the *endoxa* (popular opinions) which are the starting point in the discovery of truth.[10] Thus, Paul's starting point are the opinions of these Judean churches which he employs to prove the truthfulness of his claim; that his gospel is true reinforced by these churches. This is the primary reason for its inclusion because these axioms are the cornerstone to his entire argument.

The grammar behind the narrative also explains the Judean churches repeatedly "heard," ἀκούοντες, because "the periphrastic tense indicates a continuing activity: they kept hearing."[11] This action of repeated "hearing" by the churches were not an irregular

---

9. Martin explains, "This report implies the acceptance of Paul's gospel as valid among the churches of Judea." Martin, "Apostasy to Paganism," 447. Koptak states that "while Paul establishes this physical distance between himself and the apostles and churches, he declares a common purpose; the churches hear that Paul now preaches the faith he tried to destroy. Even while many miles separate him from the churches of Judea, he has become one with them through a common faith in the gospel. Paul has established a relationship, a consubstantiality, with Christians throughout Judea. Their praise of God on his account (1.24) indicates that Paul has become a success in his new vocation of pleasing God." Koptak, "Rhetorical Identification," 103.

10. Aristotle, *Rhet.* 1.1.11; see also *Top.* 1.1.

11. Morris, *Galatians*, 61.

Paul's Inductive Examples

activity because they kept hearing Paul preaches the same faith; for the continuation of an action (of hearing) helps substantiate the truth of an action. People are inclined and have a natural affinity to believe something is true or the semblance of it based on the repeated nature of an action. Cicero reminds us, "By example we clarify the nature of our statement, while testimony we establish its truth."[12] The churches were thoroughly convinced that Paul's change was genuine and he was no longer a persecutor of the church, thus they glorified God on his behalf (Gal 1:24). This testimony "serves as proof that they thereby acknowledge that God was behind it."[13] If God were behind the messenger and his message, it follows that his gospel message must have derived and approved by God. It was Paul's rhetorical objective to secure the beliefs of the Galatians by these authoritative testimonies, and the conclusion he wants the churches to consent to.

The Truth of the Gospel

Although the phrase "the truth of the gospel" is absent in these diminutive verses, the theme nevertheless resonates in the narrative. Albrecht Oepke explains the unique situation in which the Judean communities only heard about the gospel and became both listeners and speakers.[14] Oepke's term "Gesamtsolidarität" expresses itself in the acceptance of the Judea community that embraced Paul's gospel, it reflects a communal consent and thus the only base for God's praise, giving credence to his influence in reference to confirming Christian faith without even being present. The fact that Paul's gospel is in solidarity with the Judean churches speaks to the truth of it.[15] It is hard to convince anyone of anything without sufficient evidence.[16]

---

12. Cicero, *Rhet. Her* 4.3.5. Cicero also states that "the testimony must accord with the proposition, for otherwise it cannot confirm the proposition."
13. Tolmie, *Rhetorical Analysis*, 71.
14. Oepke, *Der Brief des Paulus an die Galater*, 67.
15. Mußner, *Der Galaterbrief*, 99.
16. Hurley, *Concise Introduction to Logic*, iii.

Induction and Example

Example Two: The Jerusalem Event (Gal 2:1–10)

> Then after fourteen years, I went up again to Jerusalem, this time with Barnabas. I took Titus along also. I went in response to a revelation and, meeting privately with those esteemed as leaders, I presented to them the gospel that I preach among the Gentiles. I wanted to be sure I was not running and had not been running my race in vain. Yet not even Titus, who was with me, was compelled to be circumcised, even though he was a Greek. This matter arose because some false believers had infiltrated our ranks to spy on the freedom we have in Christ Jesus and to make us slaves. We did not give in to them for a moment, so that the truth of the gospel might be preserved for you. As for those who were held in high esteem—whatever they were makes no difference to me; God does not show favoritism—they added nothing to my message. On the contrary, they recognized that I had been entrusted with the task of preaching the gospel to the uncircumcised, just as Peter had to the circumcised. For God, who was at work in Peter as an apostle to the circumcised, was also at work in me as an apostle to the Gentiles. James, Cephas and John, those esteemed as pillars, gave me and Barnabas the right hand of fellowship when they recognized the grace given to me. They agreed that we should go to the Gentiles, and they to the circumcised. All they asked was that we should continue to remember the poor, the very thing I had been eager to do all along.

In this pericope, Paul completes his series of grammatical markers ἔπειτα, or "then," that he first introduced in Gal 1:18, 21. Although ἔπειτα is the completion of Paul's travelogue, his description of the event in Gal 2:1 are unlike the previous two; the first two ἔπειτα establishes the chronology of his travelogue. The last adverb ἔπειτα, however, introduces a recent example, which Paul no longer attempts to prove his independence from the apostles but only the independent nature and validation of his gospel. Hunn argues that ἔπειτα in 2:1 "need not indicate the next consecutive movement but the next relevant movement."[17] Thus his argument shifts to the meeting he had with the pillar apostles and the denunciation of the false brothers.

Paul's Present Example

Aristotle recommends that we "take the examples that are appropriate to the subject and closest to the audience in time or place."[18] Analogous to Aristotle, Paul recollects a particular experience of his that ensued in Jerusalem that is similar to the disputes in Galatia. In both Jerusalem and Galatia, Paul functions as rhetor and apologist to protect the truth of the gospel against all those who oppose that truth. This event is also near in time to the Galatia situation and may have occurred less than ten years apart. Dunn explains:

> The issue of the date has usually been made to depend on the debate between the north Galatian and south Galatian hypothesis theses. Those who argue for the south Galatian hypothesis mostly do so as a way of integrating the account of Gal. 1 and 2 with the accounts in Acts. The two visits of Jerusalem of which Paul speaks in Gal. 1.18–20 and 2.1–10 are correlated with the visits of Acts 9:26–30 and 11.29–30. The result is that Galatians can be dated prior to the "Jerusalem council" of Acts 15, that is, to about AD 48 or 49. On the other hand, those who find the north Galatian hypothesis more persuasive, and who see in 4.13 a reference to two visits to (north) Galatia, have to date the letter after that second visit (presumably referred to in Acts 18.23), which means a date

---

17. Hunn, "Pleasing God or Pleasing People?," 43.
18. Aristotle, *Rhet. Alex.* 32.2.

Induction and Example

somewhere in the mid-50s. The disagreement does not amount to much.[19]

Regardless of which theory one chooses, the acceptance of either date does not diminish that Paul incorporates a narrative in proximity to the Galatian event. The Galatian community would surely interpret the event as an example since it is outside the containment of the situation that arose in Galatia.

The Rhetoric of Specification

In rhetorical speeches, if the audience were oblivious to the example text the orator should describe the paradeigma in greater detail. If the orator fails to do so, the paradeigma is subject to the audience failure to fully grasp what actually happened which prohibits them from making an informed decision in regards to their future. In our case, Paul writes the Jerusalem example under the rubric of specification because the Galatians were in all likelihood unaware of the event and the situation that surrounds the incident. The example indicates the conference occurred not within public space, but rather a private assembly among the seminal in the ecclesia (Gal 2:2). So the prospect the news would have traveled all the way to Galatia makes it implausible they would have had previous knowledge of the event. The amount of ink used to explain the character's actions and what caused the controversy bespeaks the elaborative nature of the event.[20]

To be sure, Paul could have included more elements from the Jerusalem conference, but he abstracts material fitted for the Galatian controversy. He included the example for rhetorical reasons, and therefore we must first evaluate the example under these terms, and how it relates to his initial argument. This particular event is based on three comprehensive and interrelated examples which form the one example text. The example of the uncircumcised Titus who embodies Gentile inclusion without cutting the foreskin, the

19. Dunn, *New Testament Theology*, 12.
20. Tolmie, *Rhetorical Analysis*, 77.

example of Paul who defends the gospel against the false brethren, and the cornerstone example the acceptance of Paul's gospel to the Gentiles by the pillar apostles. In each case the truth of the gospel remains the centerpiece.

Titus's Ethos: A Rhetorical Example

Paul brought Titus to Jerusalem not as a learning protégé or to evangelize those outside the faith of Christ, but rather as an example. Not merely an example, but a rhetorical example of how a Gentile is included in the community without being circumcised. The pressure to circumcise Gentiles came from the false brethren, in which Paul would reject this idea because acceptance would have been an outright dismissal of the truth of the gospel.[21] Some would conclude, however, that Paul was not forced to circumcise Titus, but he did so in hopes of not offending those Jews who were present.[22] This position is counterintuitive to the message Paul had for the churches of Galatia. It would be peculiar for Paul to say that the truth of the gospel might remain with the Galatians, but that same truth is ignored in circumcising Titus (Gal 2:5). Koptak explains the Gentiles should be welcomed into the community of Jewish believers with open arms and treated as equals without being pressed to convert over to Judaism or to be circumcised.[23]

According to Paul, he did not randomly appear in Jerusalem by his own volition nor did the pillar apostles initiate the meeting rather the driving force behind his arrival in Jerusalem was revelation. This revelatory experience probably occurred some seventeen years after his initial spiritual encounter with God that subsequently defined his gospel and mission to the Gentiles. William Walker makes an interesting point: "That Paul saw divine revelation as situational, that is, as related to specific occasions, events, problems, questions, and the like . . . the situation would likely have prompted

---

21. Ashcraft, "Paul Defends his Apostleship," 459–69.
22. Robinson, "Circumcision of Titus," see on this position 36–37.
23. Koptak, "Rhetorical Identification," 106.

Induction and Example

the revelation in the sense that the revelation was God's response to the situation."[24] Under this proposition, God knew of the circumstances that Paul's gospel faced even before he was made aware of them. The revelation brought awareness of the situation, and this may give reason why Paul brought Titus along. It is likely that discussions arose in Jerusalem whether Gentiles should become full members of the community of faith without the necessity of being circumcised, thus these matters needed Paul's presence.

In the convocation Paul did not modify his gospel with the pillar apostles as the present tense κηρύσσω ("I preach") indicates (Gal 2:2). It remained unaltered free from circumcision and Torah observance as a prerequisite to salvation. However, "By the time Paul wrote Galatians he was no longer prepared to acknowledge the authority of Jerusalem to the same extent. This is clearest in 2:6, where the change in tense in the parenthesis is best understood as indicating precisely such a change in Paul's attitude to the Jerusalem leadership—'what they once were is (now) a matter of indifference to me'; God takes no account of such evaluations of status and importance."[25] Thus Paul did not amend his gospel, but his recognition of the apostles did.

Paul and the False Brethren

The meeting in Jerusalem is not due to any triviality between Paul and the pillar apostles because they agree on the essential elements of the gospel, which he was determined to prove he was not at odds with them. The apostles never reject Paul's gospel, so the underlying consensus of his message remains one of agreement and solidarity instead of dissonance, all they require of him was to be benevolent to the poor (Gal 2:10). So, all is well, right! Actually a conflict of interest arose from individuals who questioned Paul's gospel. He explains intruders or spies snuck in and tried to infiltrate the freedom the Gentiles already had in Christ (Gal 2:4–5). The fact they

---

24. Walker, "Why Paul Went to Jerusalem," 510.
25. Dunn, "Relationship between Paul and Jerusalem," 473.

were able to voice their disagreement to the point of challenging Paul's gospel speak to the authority they had in the religious community. These intruders simply "would not grant equality to the Gentile believers. Instead, they would require circumcision, a status of bondage to their will."[26] Paul would have none of this.

Even in the context of the false brethren, Paul contends neither εἴξαμεν, or "did we yield," to their position, instead his ethos remained steadfast in declaring the truth of the gospel. The false brethren who challenged Paul's gospel did so independently of, and without the support of the Jerusalem apostles.[27] They accepted Jesus on a personal level, and believed his saving and missionary work, but they did not fully understand what that meant for Gentiles inclusion; for Gentiles to have faith in Christ simply was not enough, more was required to be full members of the family of God. They must be circumcised.

The Handshake Agreement

The question remains, why would Paul even consider consulting the pillar apostles if he did not seek their approval of his gospel? He is not ignorant to the fact that his circumcision-free gospel would be hindered without the endorsement of the Jerusalem church. Not from the standpoint he feared his gospel would be ineffective, but rather the future ramification of his Gentile ministry. Paul recognizes to "run in vain" is to "run without recognition, without fellowship, from those who should have perceived the God-given nature of Paul's mission."[28] Paul wants to establish continuity between Gentile churches and Israel; the OT prophets and Jesus' first disciples.[29] He was not trying to create a sect outside of Israel that ventured out in the wilderness on its own, but rather, he wants the truth of his gospel to be in harmony with God's mission plan to the world.

---

26. Koptak, "Rhetorical Identification," 106.
27. Ebeling, *Truth of the Gospel*, 88.
28. Robinson, "Circumcision of Titus," 27.
29. Dunn, "Relationship between Paul and Jerusalem," 468.

Induction and Example

The fact that the pillar apostles and spiritual overseers acknowledge Paul's gospel is significant, this implies they mutually recognized God was at work with Peter's mission to the Jews, and equally confirmed, and accepted, Paul's mission to the Gentiles by giving him (and Barnabas) the right hand of fellowship (Gal 2:7–8). The pillars understood "the salvation of God was one, and their task was therefore a joint-task, shared in an agreed koinonia."[30] The fact the apostles asked Paul to remember the poor is further proof they acknowledge the divine character of his gospel. It should be emphasized that Paul's rhetorical strategy was to capture the handshake agreement to inform the Galatian community that the highest religious authority in Jerusalem confirmed his circumcision free gospel which has divine origins and therefore true. It was true when he first proclaimed it, and still remains true as validated before the apostles. As indicated earlier, there are no hints in the narrative that suggest the pillars were endorsing Paul's apostleship or Paul tried to gain personal recognition or defend his status as an apostle. If we keep the example text as a rhetorical text, for the Galatians' sake, and not Paul's own apostolic identification, we will remove the complications that Paul was trying to defend his apostleship. It is not that his apostleship is on trial, but rather the legitimacy of his gospel.

The Truth of the Gospel

The agitators in Galatia threaten the Galatians' freedom by stipulating to be true followers of Christ they must be circumcised. Similarly, the false brethren in Jerusalem tried to contravene Paul's circumcision-free gospel and the freedom they had in Christ (Gal 2:4). I am unclear, therefore, why H. Alan Brehm concludes the false brethren in Jerusalem are identical with the agitators in Galatia.[31] This interpretive lens ignores the function of the example, and thus disempowers Paul's rhetoric. Their agenda and motives are similar, but their identity, time, and space are different.

---

30. Robinson, "Circumcision of Titus," 25.
31. Brehm, "Paul's Relationship with the Jerusalem Apostles," 11–16.

Paul's Inductive Examples

In both narratives, the truth of the gospel is synonymous with Christian freedom. The agitators and the false brothers argue on the basis of exclusivism, and Paul argues on the basis of inclusiveness, which means the truth of the gospel is freedom from the obligations of circumcision and Torah law. Ebeling correctly states, "if circumcision is made a condition necessary for salvation, it contradicts the unconditional nature of Christ's grace. The Torah remains the universal source of salvation; Christ is incorporated into it, where he is admitted as a mere supplementary datum."[32] Before Christ Torah and cutting the foreskin were essential to a relationship with God, but after his arrival, Christ is now fundamental to having relationship with God.[33] One can argue, if Paul had spurned the opportunity to speak in defense of Christian freedom, and the universal nature of the gospel of grace, one could "imagine the theological and historical consequences of a careless surrender in this case!"[34] It would also set a theological precedent for generations to come that Gentiles must be circumcised in order to be accepted into the community of believers. Gentiles are only made free from the external rite of circumcision, which induces slavery through Christ, and in Christ alone.

Example Three: The Antiochian Event (Gal 2:11-14)[35]

> When Cephas came to Antioch, I opposed him to his face, because he stood condemned. For before certain men

---

32. Ebeling, *Truth of the Gospel*, 96.
33. Ebeling, *Truth of the Gospel*, 99.
34. Ebeling, *Truth of the Gospel*, 98.
35. Martyn explains, "The first church to arise in one of the truly great metropolitan centers of the Roman Empire, the Antioch congregation was a community of some means, able to assemble funds for the church in Jerusalem. It also became the initial testing ground for the formula that speaks of two parallel lines of mission, one to the Jews and one to the Gentiles vv. 7, 9. Its major leaders, Barnabas and Paul, were Jews by birth in Acts; all of the named leaders in Antioch were Jews (Gal 2:12-14). Yet, it had an active

Induction and Example

came from James, he used to eat with the Gentiles. But when they arrived, he began to draw back and separate himself from the Gentiles because he was afraid of those who belonged to the circumcision group. The other Jews joined him in his hypocrisy, so that by their hypocrisy even Barnabas was led astray. When I saw that they were not acting in line with the truth of the gospel, I said to Cephas in front of them all, "You are a Jew, yet you live like a Gentile and not like a Jew. How is it, then, that you force Gentiles to follow Jewish customs?"

Like example two, Paul recollects an event from his recent past in Antioch that is apropos to the situation that arose in Galatia. Here Paul abruptly shift gears from the previous narrative without the luxury of a transitional sentence or using the literary formula "for example" or "for instance," which introduces the example. He does leave grammatical evidence, however, he is employing a paradigmatic event using the Greek time adverb Ὅτε, or "when," to indicate an action of the past (2:11). Gaventa is correct in saying that "the shift from ἔπειτα to οτε δε signals a shift in events."[36] The shift of context is another strong indication that a paradeigma is being used. Like the previous two examples, this example is a dependent rhetorical unit and does not have a life of its own and is only a part of a whole. The purpose and inclusion of the event can only be confirmed, and traced to the propositio/causa—sub propositio (1:6–9, 10–12).

---

mission to Gentiles, pursued mainly by Barnabas and Paul, and resulting in a mixed congregation clearly distinct from the local synagogues. Mixed as it was, it was different, in fact, not only from its neighboring synagogues and from the church in Jerusalem. It was also different from those of its daughter churches that were drawn solely from Gentiles. In short, this congregation of born Jews and born Gentiles was more than interesting. It was a sort of time bomb, being the locus in which the two parallel lines of mission threatened to cross in such a way as to pose unexpected problems." Martyn, *Galatians*, 232.

36. Gaventa, "Galatians 1 and 2," 317.

Paul's Inductive Examples

The Rhetoric of Brevity

In Gal 1:13, Paul speaks of his persecution in brevity, "You have heard of my previous way of life in Judaism, how intensely I persecuted the church of God and tried to destroy it." Since the Galatians were already aware of Paul's persecution of the church, it was unnecessary to disclose why he did so because it would have added no rhetorical value. All he needed to say is that it happened nothing more and nothing less. The nondisclosure of the specifics of Paul's persecution in this verse, and the following three verses are extraneous to the Galatians controversy; he brought this external material in to argue the causa.[37] The persecution Paul briefly mentions in 1:23, is also external and unrelated to the issues that arose in Galatia. He wanted the Galatians to know the Judean churches preached the same "faith" as he did.[38]

---

37. Paul was not egoistic in speaking about his credentials, his brief recollection here sets the stage for the first half of the contrast. He wanted the Galatians to know he had no reason to break away from the traditions of his fathers because he was faring well advancing more than others. Nothing in his fervor for God, and Judaism, recommended that a change was necessary. On all accounts, however, he was a religious extremist that took his injudicious enthusiasm to preserve his Judaic traditions and convictions. He went out of his way to get authorization from the high priest to pursue, and persecute any who followed this Way (Acts 22:4; 26:9-11). If a person or a group of individuals believe they are doing the will of God by using force that may cause bodily harm, in order for a person or community to abandon their faith or belief, this religious fervor is not of God. In Acts 9:4, Jesus said: "Saul, Saul, why do you persecute me?" The second half of the contrast, Paul would have them know his gospel did not originate from any human, he was set aside from birth (although the call came later in its proper season) to proclaim the gospel to Gentiles. He informs us, he did not go up to Jerusalem to consult the apostles but traveled to Arabia (where it is assumed he received revelations from Christ) and then returned to Damascus. Thus, his rhetorical strategy was to make known that his gospel can be traced back to God, and not man, and therefore the Galatians should accept his previous proclamation as true (1:17-20).

38. Nowhere in the letter is it suggested the Galatians suffered some form of persecution for their faith. If they did suffer persecution, it is not Paul's starting point for the truth of the gospel. The truth of the gospel, and the examples that disclosed the subject, are about how Gentiles are identified, and how they are justified by faith without being circumcised. The theme of persecution mentioned in 5:11 is an accusation or criticism against Paul that

Induction and Example

With that being said, the current pericope scholars have devoted considerable interest in this brief narrative probably because it offers a glimpse into the history of the early church. Paul is less enthused in writing church history because it was beyond his rhetorical objective to do so, he only gives his readers and auditors the details as it relates to the Galatians' controversy, offering an abridged version of the example leaving out dispensable information. The Galatians would have contextualized the event and made the necessary inference that Paul argues for the truth of the gospel similarly to the crisis in Galatians (2:14). They gleaned from his experience that the dispute surrounds table fellowship that caused the crisis, and the arrival of men from James and the circumcision group initiated the response from Peter (2:12).

Some interpreters would argue that since Paul controlled the rhetoric of the event, it is surprising he left out certain details and actions. On one end of the spectrum, if Paul was victorious in his conflict with Peter, it would be to his advantage to include his response and the outcome of the event, to strengthen his claim for the truth of the gospel; see even the esteemed Peter agreed to the divine origin of my gospel, and now I have further proof that my gospel is true. On the other, Paul left out particular details that were to his disadvantage. If Peter was victorious in his conflict with Paul; Paul saw fit to exclude the outcome because it would have weakened his argument for the truth of the gospel among the Galatians community, and therefore he omitted Peter's response for rhetorical reasons.

---

he once preached circumcision, perhaps in reference to his circumcision of Timothy, Acts 16:3. He explains, if I preached circumcision that would naturally cancel out being persecuted. Under this consideration, "the offense of the cross has been abolished." See Morris, *Galatians*, 161–62, for the various views on this verse. In 6:12, Paul accuses those who tried to avoid persecution would do so at the expense of the cross of Christ. It is worth mentioning, Paul did not persecute the church because the Gentiles were not circumcised, he persecuted the church, as Hultgren explains, "because they belong to 'the Way' (9:2; 22:4); he is involved in 'opposing the name of Jesus of Nazareth' (26:9); and he tries 'to make them blaspheme'" (26:11). He explains further that "it is understood by him as a heterodox movement within Judaism which ought to be opposed and brought back into line with 'normative Judaism.'" Hultgren, "Paul's Pre-Christian Persecution," 100.

I contend, however, this rhetoric has no relevance because it has no bearing on the nature of the example. If we take Paul at his word that he testified to the independent nature of his gospel beforehand with an oath (Gal 1:20), it is strange that he flippantly forged the truth of the events that followed (Gal 1:21—2:14). The narrative explains that Peter was eating with Gentiles without any reservations, but he removed himself from table fellowship out of fear of the circumcision group, and according to Paul, he was acting out of character of his true convictions. If we take this into consideration, Peter was already in possession of the truth of the gospel for Gentile inclusion (he just failed to uphold that truth because the influence of others), therefore Paul had no need to express Peter's response or even if Peter had a response to Paul's admonishment. We are reminded that Peter accepted and ate with Cornelius a Gentile, and his household, after receiving a vision from God (Acts 10). Peter did not require Cornelius to be proselytized. Nevertheless, the issue that was most important to Paul was his stance against the truth of the gospel.

The Antiochian Dispute

Philip Esler maintains the dispute in Antioch was caused because the Gentiles had to be circumcised to participate in table fellowship.[39] Witherington asserts that Peter regularly ate with the Gentiles in Antioch without any reservations, thus the church in Jerusalem (learned of his behavior) sent representatives to speak with him, thus causing him to pull back from table fellowship.[40] Martyn believes "the issue of circumcision was not reopened [from the Jerusalem council because] the issue was changed to the matter of Jewish Gentile association at meals."[41] Dunn on the other hand contends the issues arose in Antioch because:

---

39. Esler, "Making and Breaking an Agreement," 286.
40. Witherington, *Grace in Galatia*, 149.
41. Martyn, "Galatians," 233.

Induction and Example

The men from James however were shocked at what seemed to them a minimal level of Torah observance and a far too casual and unacceptable attitude to the Torah. They would no doubt point out that the earlier agreement made in Jerusalem had in no way changed the obligations to Torah obedience resting on the Jewish believer, and must have insisted that the Jewish believers in Antioch conduct themselves with greater discipline and greater loyalty to the Torah, more like their fellow believers in Palestine and with a similar regard for the heritage of Jewish tradition and custom.[42]

The issue that arose in Antioch probably had more to do with how these Gentiles were to be identified than the dietary requirements or Torah observance. Unless Paul's analogy is defective, this example is consistent with issues concerning circumcision and the identity crisis the Galatians were experiencing. Mark Nanos correctly states "that the ones advocating circumcision had nothing to do with the food being eaten or with the fact that it was being eaten with Gentiles, and it was not the threat of impurity or idolatry either. Rather, it was the way these Gentiles were being identified at these meals."[43] Those advocating circumcision interpreted the event as Jews and Gentiles were identified as equals in the community of faith; this was an unacceptable practice. Eric Stewart contends, "If Paul was concerned about the food or the manner in which it was eaten, it seems likely that he would have addressed such concerns, as he does in 1 Corinthians 8 and 10, where he addresses both the type of food and the contexts in which it was eaten."[44] If Paul were truly interested in stressing kosher meals as a principle concern in Antioch, it is unclear why he neglects to elaborate on this very issue here and in Galatians as a whole.

---

42. Dunn, "Incident at Antioch," 35–36.
43. Nanos, "What Was at Stake," 316.
44. Stewart, "I'm Okay, You're Not Okay," 6.

Paul's Inductive Examples

Pathos

Although ancillary to the overarching theme of the paradeigma, there are several distinctive analogies that are integrated within the proof and the most telling are Peter's fearfulness and cowardice, and Paul's confidence. Whereas Paul's ethos is surely exhibited, Peter's actions are largely motivated by all three proofs: pathos, logos and ethos. Peter, who is duly noted as one of the original twelve apostles and, one who had an intimate relationship with Jesus of Nazareth, and was known for his bravado in the past, defaults from his previous theological position out of fear of the circumcision group. This fear Peter possessed was not a feeble emotional response to the event because "the actual term used ('he was afraid' *phoboumenos*) suggests a rather stronger emotional reaction and makes it plausible that there was more to the message from James [or the circumcision group]."[45] The group of individuals that motivated such an emotional response were powerful enough to influence Peter's behavior, even to the point he removed himself from eating with Gentiles.

Even though Peter's fear is underscored, his pathe response is not deadened to intellectual inquiry. The fear Peter experienced is part of his intellectualization of the state of events and realizing the consequences thereof, and as a result, deviates from his previous theological convictions. Steven J. Kraftchick states that "fear can cause us to consider what to do to avoid the circumstances that have created the emotion."[46] Aristotle labels emotions as "all those affections which cause men to change their opinion in regard to their judgments, and are accompanied by pleasure and pain."[47] If Peter disregarded the words (whatever they were) from the circumcision group and continued to eat and fellowship with Gentiles, it would certainly have affected his ministry or apostolic standing among the Jews. He weighed the options: to remain loyal to the truth of the gospel, and his personal experience with God in regard

---

45. Fung, *Epistle to the Galatians*, 108.
46. Kraftchick, "Πάθη in Paul," 45.
47. Aristotle, *Rhet*, 2.1.8.

Induction and Example

to that truth, or remain loyal to man's religious truth and traditions, he chose the latter. This is the very reason Paul calls Peter a servant of men because he tried to please them.

Opposite to fear is confidence. Aristotle asserts, "The orator persuades by moral character when his speech is delivered in such a manner as to render him worthy of confidence; for we feel confidence in a greater degree and more readily in persons of worth in regard to everything in general."[48] In the case of Paul, he does not succumb to Peter's eminence as a leading apostle but rather with full confidence confronts him when the truth of the gospel is at stake. His willingness to stand alone among Jewish Christians, and confront Peter, suggest that he saw Peter as his equal.[49] A person who has confidence comes from the assurance knowing that something one holds to or believe is right. Paul had the utmost confidence because he believes his gospel is true, and he was unwilling to relinquish that truth for no one. This demonstrates how deeply rooted, and dedicated, Paul was to his divine gospel that he even indicted Peter and Barnabas.

Taylor believes that Paul's actions severely impaired his apostolic standing in the ecclesia. He states:

> It is generally recognized that his confrontation with Peter radically altered Paul's standing in the Antiochean church, as well as resulting in the termination of his partnership with Barnabas. Just how cataclysmic this event was for Paul has not been fully appreciated, however. This is largely because scholarship has been unwilling to acknowledge just how bound up Paul's life and work had been with the church of Antioch. He had derived dyadic identity through his membership of that community, and his commission as an apostle had derived

---

48. Aristotle, *Rhet*, 1.2.

49. Witherington, *Grace in Galatia*, 151–52. He also states, "In such an important matter James was not likely to send someone who was not known and respected by Peter so that the instructions would be with the utmost seriousness. It is interesting, however, and perhaps important that Paul does not call these persons false brothers who came from James. He treats them with more respect perhaps, than the false brothers."

Paul's Inductive Examples

also from the Antiochean church. Separation from that community would therefore have entailed the loss both of dyadic identity and of apostolic commission, including any jurisdiction over the churches of Galatia.[50]

Despite the possible negative impact it may have had on Paul's ministry, he remained steadfast unwavering in his convictions that the truth of the gospel must remain. As a matter of fact, "The same instinctive courage that drove Paul to risk his skin by rebuking a bad man, Elymas, in front of the Proconsul drove him to risk his standing in the church by correcting a good man, Peter, the greatly loved and honored, in front of them all."[51] Thus Paul remained bold and courageous to confront Peter despite the presence of those who came from James and the circumcision group.

Ethos

Even though Paul's primary intent was not to injure Peter's character in the example, the incident nevertheless reveals Peter's ethos as a consequence of his actions. Garver explains that "all examples have emotional and ethical colorings" and "all examples reveal character, whether intentionally or not."[52] To spare and circumvent his admonishment of Peter would have compromised the core of the event. The example only comes to the forefront and included as proofs because of Peter's ethical and theological response to the circumcision group.

Nevertheless, viewing the calm before the storm, the narrative implies that nothing interrupted the kosher relationship between Peter and the Antiochian community. All the dietary restrictions and food laws between Jews and Gentiles that separated the two ethnic groups were extraneous. As the narrative explains, Peter was initially comfortable "eating with the Gentiles" without any reservations, because the verb συνήσθιεν (he was eating) "expresses

---

50. Taylor, "Paul's Apostolic Legitimacy," 69.
51. Pollock, *Apostle: A Life of Paul*, 102.
52. Garver, *Aristotle's Rhetoric*, 157–58.

Induction and Example

the habitual action of the past: he used to eat regularly."[53] But after the men from James arrive, and in particular the circumcision group, the storm appears, and Peter's ethos morphs from one that includes Gentiles to one that excludes them. Paul renders Peter's behavior disingenuous because the actual word he employs "[συνυπεκρίθησαν] indicates 'to answer from under' and refers to actors who, in playing a part, spoke from under a mask. The actors hid their true selves behind the role they were playing. The word indicates the concealment of wrong feelings, character, under the pretense of better ones."[54] Thus, out of cowardice, Peter went against his own conscious and judgment.[55] Every so often, when we are in public space and confronted with hard decisions our judgments are contrary to what we truly believe, although the right decision is in our possession, we decide to rebel against what we truly believe.[56]

The event expresses the influential power of Peter's ethos, his behavior emboldens Barnabas and other members of the Jewish community to embrace his theological position. Peter must have been recognized as a leading authority not only in Jerusalem, but this recognition extended to the Antiochian community. Bengt Holmberg argues that Peter's halakic authority controlled the behavior of these believers in Paul's district in Antioch.[57] Paul certainly would have expected alliance from his fellow Gentile missionary, Barnabas, who witnessed that Gentile believers were not required to be circumcised upon entry into the new community during their first missionary journey. Barnabas nevertheless still felt compelled to side with Peter on this matter.[58]

---

53. Rogers and Rogers, *New Linguistic and Exegetical Key*, 424.

54. Rogers and Rogers, *New Linguistic and Exegetical Key*, 424. See Burton, *Galatians*; Guthrie, *Galatians*; Kittel and Friedrich, *TDNT*; and Spicq, *TLNT*.

55. Holmberg, *Paul and Power*, 32.

56. Leighton, "Aristotle and the Emotions," 208.

57. He states that "by halakic authority is meant the power to promulgate authoritative and normative teaching of a doctrinal, ethical, and legal nature." Holmberg, *Paul and Power*, 34.

58. It should be noted that "Barnabas had brought Paul into the fellowship of believers in Jerusalem when those believers were all afraid of him, doubting the reality of his conversion (Acts 9:26–28). And it was Barnabas who brought

Paul's Inductive Examples

Concerning Paul's ethos, Vos asserts that Paul's character derives directly from the gospel.[59] He was so entrenched in the gospel he proclaimed it would be virtually impossible to separate the person from the message. The same intensity and energy he devoted as a starch Pharisee, he continued in his dedication to Christ. Paul's ethos can be described: (1) Paul's apostolic calling in Gal 1:1, (2) his trust in God and not in man in Gal 1:10–12, (3) the certainty that his gospel was true in Gal 2:7–10; 4:16, (4) his relationship with the crucified Christ in Gal 2:20, (5) Paul's ethos is not restricted to his bold confrontation with Peter, the same boldness he displayed against the agitators for the truth of the gospel in Galatians.

The Truth of the Gospel

The stand Paul had against the false brethren in Jerusalem is theological consistent with his stand against Peter and Barnabas and the Jewish believers of Antioch.[60] Like the Jerusalem convocation, Paul includes the Antioch episode because he believes the truth of the gospel was "once again endangered in Galatia."[61] Russell also points out:

> The truth of the gospel also had specific application to Jewish Christians who still attempted to live Torah-observant lives (e.g., Cephas, Barnabas, and the rest, vv. 11–14). The gospel eliminated the barrier that Torah-observance created between Jewish and Gentile Christians for four reasons. (1) Neither Jew nor Gentile is justified by keeping the Law, but only through faith in Christ (vv. 15–16). (2) Being justified through faith in Christ apart from Torah-observance does not make Jewish

---

Paul into the church at Antioch (Acts 11:25–26) and Barnabas who worked with Paul on the poor saints there (Acts 11:30), and Barnabas who worked with Paul on the first missionary journey (Acts 13:2[—14:28]). So it is not surprising that Paul evidently took this man's defection very hard." Morris, *Galatians*, 80.

59. Vos, "Paul's Argumentation in Galatians," 10.
60. Taylor, "Paul's Apostolic Legitimacy," 76.
61. Garland, "Paul's Defense of the Truth of the Gospel," 165.

Induction and Example

> Christians like nonobservant Gentile "sinners" because no one can be judged as a "transgressor" (παραβάτην) of the Law if he is not required to obey it (vv. 17–18). ... (3) Jewish Christians died to the Law and live to God because of their cocrucifixion with Christ, which applied His substitutionary death to them to free them from the bodily constraints of the Law on them (Gal. 2:19–20). (4) If Jewish Christians nullify (ἀθετῶ) the universal nature of the gospel (τὴν χάριν τοῦ Θεοῦ) by emphasizing Torah-observance, then Christ died needlessly (2:21).[62]

Paul a devoted apologist for the truth of the gospel believes one is not justified by the works of the law, nor does he believe works are the ruling power over one's life in Christ. He believes Peter's actions sent the wrong message for "the effect of his withdrawal from table-fellowship with Gentiles must have been to make Gentile Christians think that they were regarded as at best second-class citizens in the church-that they were regarded, in fact, much as Gentile God-fearers were regarded by the synagogue. If the Gentile mission was to make progress, this situation must be cleared up."[63] Thus, a sharp rebuke was in order for the esteemed Peter.

Example Four: The Faith of Abraham (Gal 3:6–9)

> So also Abraham "believed God, and it was credited to him as righteousness." Understand, then, that those who faith are children of Abraham. Scripture foresaw that God would justify the Gentiles by faith, and announced the gospel in advance to Abraham: "All nations will be blessed through you." So those who rely on faith are blessed along with Abraham, the man of faith.

---

62. Russell, "Rhetorical Analysis," 424.
63. Bruce, "Galatian Problems," 309.

Paul's Inductive Examples

In example four, Paul bypasses a time marker and instead employs the adverb καθώς, "even as" or "just as," to introduce the historical example. The historical example is an event and action performed by a particular individual(s) in the distant past. Paul ushers in the Abrahamic narrative to argue his causa, and to counter respond to the agitators' usage of him in Gal 1:6–9.

Typically a strong indication that a historical paradeigma is employed one will recognize the grammatical combination of a past tense action and a present tense action.[64] In reviewing Abraham's paradeigma, the past-tense action is known and completed (Abraham's faith), the present-tense action of the Galatians is still occuring, that is, they are presently or are on the verge of changing their beliefs, and the future-tense action is unknown pending the Galatians' response to Paul's letter. In the example of the great king (contemporary) in Aristotle's Rhetoric, he employs a sequence of the biographies of Darius and Xerxes (historical examples) instead of their total antiquities.[65] In like manner, Paul does not probe into the aggregate biography of the patriarch Abraham, nor randomly chosen events such as his test of faith with Lot or the details of the attempted sacrifice of Isaac, which is inconsequential to his rhetorical argument (Gen 13; 22:17). Instead, he employs three selective motifs constituted for the Galatians' controversy; namely, Abraham *believed*, *received a promise*, and was *blessed* by God.[66]

These threefold themes are sequential in which the promise and the blessing of God sprung from Abraham's belief that God would multiple his decedents as the stars in heaven Gen 15:1–5. Sam K. Williams concludes: "Abraham believed God as the deity revealed his purpose in a particular word, the promise of descendants as numerous as the stars of heaven (Gen 15:1–5). Similarly, the Christian believes God as he has revealed his purpose in a particular word, the gospel of Christ crucified (Gal 3:1). For both

---

64. Lyons, "Exemplum," 26.

65. Lyons, "Exemplum," 31.

66. See Abraham's interaction with God in Gen 12:1–5; 15:1–16; 17:1–19; 18:1–33. Each time Abraham experienced God, his knowledge of God increased.

Induction and Example

Abraham and the Christian the experience of life in faith begins on the God-ward side, for God takes the initiative and sets the redemptive event in motion."[67] The Galatians did not know God under the auspices of paganism, nor did they seek out God's favor (Gal 4:8), their response to God came through Paul's proclamation of Christ (not through the acceptance of Torah law or cutting the foreskin), and his circumcision free gospel.

Our primary text the historical example begins in Gal 3:6, where Paul applies Abraham as an exemplary figure of faith and hearing based on the narrative and syntax of Gal 3:5, serving as a syntactical and rhetorical link to 3:6, and ultimately reaches back to Gal 1:6-9. Terri H. Neuman states, "The gentile converts received the Spirit as a gift in connection with their hearing with faith (3:2—past tense, apparently referring to their conversion). They continue to experience the gift of the Spirit in the same way (3:5—present tense, pointing to an ongoing experience)."[68] Here Paul compares Abraham hearing God's voice and responding in faith with the Galatians hearing his message about Christ and responding in faith.[69] Witherington concludes similarly that "καθὼς does not refer forward, but rather backward being conceptually dependent on vs. 5."[70] Since the historical example is an analogy between the past and present, it would be peculiar to denote the Galatians hearing with faith, without meaning the same type of hearing Abraham experienced. Both fall under the same class of hearing and believing. Hearing God's voice and responding in faith, was the foremost reason Abraham was justified by faith and considered righteous before God. Williams also states,

> Paul is pointing to the similarity of Abraham's experience and the Galatians experience. . . . Abraham's believing

---

67. Williams, "Justification and the Spirit in Galatians," 93.

68. Neuman, "Paul's Appeal to the Experience of the Spirit," 61.

69. Richard Hayes, contends, however, that "the accent in verse 5 falls heavily upon the action of God, who 'supplies the Spirit and works miracles,' and ἐξ ἀκοῆς πίστεως must therefore be understood to mean through the proclamation of [the] faith." Hayes, *Faith of Jesus*, 170.

70. Witherington, *Grace in Galatia*, 218.

Paul's Inductive Examples

> was a response to God's speaking. This response was, in the first place, a kind of hearings and the word which Abraham heard came from God. Hearing is always a passive act, for that which is heard always comes from beyond the self. At the same time, hearing is always active; it requires attentiveness, alertness, appropriation. . . . In light of the parallels between Abraham's experience and the Galatians' which Paul appears to be stressing in Gal. 3.5–6, it seems likely that the *kathos* which introduces v. 6 is intended to indicate similarity. . . . Thus Paul's argument moves from the Galatians' experience to Abraham's in this way: "Does He who supplies the Spirit to you and works wonders among you do so on the basis of works of the Law or the hearing of faith?" (The unavoidable, but unexpressed, response anticipated from the Galatians would be: "He does so, of course, *ex akoès pisteōs*").[71]

Paul does not intend through rhetorical techniques to have the Galatians merely draw the inference between Abraham's past experience of faith and their own; his aim is to convince them they are already the children of Abraham regardless of whether they adhere to Torah law.

Paul as an Interpreter of (History) Scripture

In all probability the Abrahamic argument originated with the agitators, in which they used selective scriptures in Genesis (e.g., circumcision and the divine covenant) that testify against Paul's circumcision free gospel. Needless to say, Paul responds to the agitators by undermining their argument and proof-texting from scripture using his own Abrahamic proofs. Kraftchick states more on the possible position of the agitators:

> Apparently the missionaries arguments that ritual behaviors were the next step toward deeper allegiance to God and that they were a necessary part of Christian existence made sense both on a logical and theological plane. Scripture showed that God's promise of blessing

---

71. Williams, "Justification and the Spirit in Galatians," 93.

Induction and Example

was made to Abraham and his descendants (3:14–18), so it must have seemed both logical and correct to conclude that receiving the blessing promised to Abraham meant that one must become a descendent of him. Circumcision as a sign of belonging to the covenant people, would have appeared quite proper.[72]

Undoubtedly, Paul's knowledge of Torah and scripture puts him in the position to aggressively respond to the agitators' claim. On so many fronts, Paul functions more as an exegete, a rhetor than he does as a pastor. Even though Paul manipulates scripture and act as a rhetor, he "does not change this history, nor does he offer an alternative history. What he does do, is to show . . . what was always there, but what was never properly realized or what has become hidden in the course of Torah-centric revision of Israel's past."[73] Thus, Paul is not trying to debunk Abraham in light of new evidence but to demystify Gentile's status in salvation history. To be sure, Paul's exegesis and ingenuity stretches the boundaries of traditional understanding of Abraham in salvation history, as Hansen points out: "In contrast to the use of Abraham in much contemporary Jewish literature, Paul dissociates the Abrahamic promise and its blessing from the law and works of the law. This dissociation is designed to explode any attempt to use Abraham as an example for circumcision and law-observance."[74] This fresh perspective of the patriarch Abraham turns the agitators' paradeigma of Abraham on its head, and reinterpret it so that everyone who has faith in Christ could gain salvation in God without being circumcised.

Law and Faith/Promise

Like other themes of the letter, Paul describes the antithesis between the law and faith not with the intent to disqualify the purpose of the law, he seeks to establish that "there can no longer be a coexistence of faith in Christ with fulfilling the requirements of the

72. Kraftchick, "Πάθη in Paul," 59.
73. Lategan, "Paul's Use of History," 128.
74. Silva, "Abraham, Faith, and Works," 256. Silva cites Hansen.

Paul's Inductive Examples

law because the law/Torah no longer has any constitutive significance for one's relation to God."[75] Susan Liubinskas correctly states that "the Law is not intrinsically inferior, since it has a divine origin. Rather, it is functionally inferior due to its temporary nature and indirect reception."[76] E. P. Sanders also makes the point the argument in this section has more to do with Christian missionaries than Judaism; it is not attempting to highlight faith or works per se, but rather the view that Gentiles must accept Mosaic law as a precondition to salvation to be truly recognized as sons of Abraham.[77] He further concludes that "the subject of Galatians is not whether or not humans, abstractly conceived. Can by good deeds earn enough merit to be declared righteous at the judgment?"[78] Sanders is correct that the primary dispute in Galatians is not how one can gain inheritance by earning brownie points or following every aspect of the law.

The principal issue therefore in Galatians has more to do with how these Gentiles are to be identified. Liubinskas stresses that "Paul is not simply interested in ensuring that the believers in Galatia have a correct understanding of the law and its function. He is also seeking to ensure that they have a proper understanding of who they are in Christ."[79] Paul's argument rest on the fact that these Galatian Gentiles are not identified by the law but faith in Christ (Gal 3:26–29). T. David Gordon asserts:

> One can now see that Paul's polemic at Galatia may best be understood as a polemic regarding identity symbols. Shall the people of God be identified by Torah or by Christ? Which symbol is appropriate for the present redemptive-historical circumstances? The polemic is not in the first place soteriological (that is, faith or works as instrument of justification) but eschatological (whether God has fulfilled the promises to Abraham by means of

---

75. Schnelle, *Apostle Paul*, 282–83.
76. Liubinskas, "Identification by the Spirit Alone," 33.
77. Sanders, *Paul, the Law, and the Jewish People*, 19.
78. Sanders, *Paul, the Law, and the Jewish People*, 18.
79. Liubinskas, "Identification by Spirit Alone," 28.

Induction and Example

the Christ-event) and, by consequence, ecclesiological (whether the believing Gentiles are in fact full members of the covenant community).[80]

Circumcision is no longer an identity marker particularly for the new eschatological community because circumcision is equivalent to nothing in Christ (Gal 5:2–3, 6). The Galatians by remaining uncircumcised are the eschatological community turning to God triggered by the death and resurrection of Jesus Christ.[81] Thus, in Paul's theology, circumcision is a meaningless ritual that has no bearing on becoming full members of the family of God; Christ and the Spirit are the new identity markers as implied in Gal 3:1–5. Neither circumcision nor uncircumcision means anything; what counts is a new creation (Gal 6:17). If the Galatians decide to reject Paul's exhortation and become circumcised Christ would have profited them nothing, and they would uphold the identity of a Jew; but Paul would have none of this.

The Truth of the Gospel

Although the phrase "the truth of the gospel" does not appear in the Abrahamic narrative, the theme nevertheless resonates in Paul's theology, as Gordon explains: "Nothing less than the 'truth of the gospel' is at stake . . . because at the heart of the gospel is God's faithfulness to the promises made to Abraham. The very essence of Paul's gospel consists in the declaration that in Christ God has indeed fulfilled the promises he made with Abraham, to bless 'all the nations' in him."[82] The agitators who put regulations on the universal nature of Paul's gospel mandate that the Galatians be circumcised as a prerequisite of salvation in Christ. Paul's theology of Christ, however, is inclusive which opens the door to all nations without the necessity of being circumcised.

---

80. Gordon, "Problem at Galatia," 40.
81. Kahl, *Galatians Re-imagined*, 222.
82. Gordon, *Problem at Galatia*, 43.

Paul's Inductive Examples

In Rom 16:25–26, Paul states, "Now to him who is able to establish you in accordance with my gospel, the message I proclaim about Jesus Christ, in keeping with the revelation of the mystery hidden for long ages past, but now revealed and made known through the prophetic writings by the command of the eternal God, so that all the Gentiles might come to the obedience that comes from faith." There is nothing new in Paul's gospel, it remains in harmony with the ages of the past, but his gospel also looks to the eschaton. Paul safeguards these truisms of the truth of the gospel.

Conclusion

IN NT LITERATURE, SCHOLARS are inclined to devote more attention to deductive arguments than examples. This is unsurprising because even Aristotle focuses more on enthymemes than he does rhetorical examples. Be that as it may, the example is ubiquitous in the biblical corpus appearing in various forms, namely, historical examples, present examples, personal examples, and analogy (parables). In the first two chapters, I focus mainly on induction and Aristotle's rhetorical example. In inductive theory, if there is a relationship that exist between two experiences of the same kind, and another experience of the same kind, we make an inductive inference that these experiences are somehow related. These experiences are not vacant of thought, rather it is the mind, the ability to grasp and understand the nature of things. Aristotle uses the historical example as a rhetorical devise to persuade the audience to think otherwise of a particular position, in this sense the example is customarily associated with deliberative oration because the future every so often resemble the past.

In the subsequent two chapters, I employ the concept of induction and example to analyze biblical text. The inductive process

Induction and Example

(observation and experience) offer insight into how biblical authors and their communities formed their beliefs about the nature and identity of Jesus. I assert moreover that the example is not free standing text, but contingent text that produce meaning from other text. The biblical writer employs the historical, present, and personal example as a rhetorical devise to support a proposition or sub-topic. In the last two chapters, Paul's examples function as supporting evidence to the causa, these examples are used to persuade the Galatians that his gospel is true and the agitators' gospel is false. His personal examples are similar to the Galatian controversy, in which they establish a universal principle, the truth of the gospel. This truth is liberty from paganism and the bondage of the law. We should note, Paul's skills as a rhetor should not be overlooked, even if one argues that Paul was not formally trained in the art of rhetoric, one must acknowledge he had rhetorical skills beyond the rudimentary level, he certainly had the artistic skills to employ a variety of examples that are germane to situation that arose in Galatia.

Appendix

A Brief Survey of the Scholarship on Aristotle's First Principles

PHILOSOPHERS, LOGICIANS, AND SCHOLARS often debate Aristotle's concept of induction. The opposing viewpoints arise because it is problematic to trace Aristotle's induction to a single entity, although scholars have tried to systematize induction.[1] The question that further presses the interpreter is whether the process of induction emerges from Aristotle's first principles, which originate in thought through sensory organs, or whether these principles come from dialectical arguments. Allan Bäck holds that "we get at, or discover, candidates for first principles through a messy process involving direct observation of phenomenon and generalization therefrom as well as through a critique of current views in the field."[2] T. H. Irwin believes grasping first principles takes a combination of dialectical arguments and common beliefs, but he concludes that observation and experience give an account of right first principles.[3]

1. Pedersen, "More on Aristotelian Epagoge," 301–19.
2. Bäck, "Aristotle's Discovery of First Principles," 163.
3. Irwin, "Aristotle's Discovery of Metaphysics," 212.

Appendix

Groarke believes, however, that dialectic endoxa participate in apprehending first principles, but he does not conclude that endoxa are the starting point in grasping these principles. He explains further that "we do not use propositions to prove first principles; rather we use first principles to prove propositions."[4] Before we explain a phenomenon or why something is the case, we must first observe and experience it inductively. We cannot argue that global warming causes destructive climate change and caused by human activity such as the release of greenhouse gasses unless scientists first induce from empirical investigation and other inductive methods that this is the case. The process of induction supplies first principles, and we cannot explain first principles because there is nothing prior to them.[5]

It stands to reason that "even if the endoxa are true, they do not qualify as science. Science requires more than having a true opinion, it requires an explanation or account."[6] Aristotle's first principles do not precede induction, but rather have inductive origins, and therefore indemonstrable in form. One may ask, "Where does induction begin? It begins, not with arguments, not even with words, but with concepts."[7] Once scientific discovery is comprehensive then we attempt to substantiate our hypotheses in argumentative form.

Sense Perception

If we agree that first principles are ascertained by induction, the next questions to consider are what is sense perception and do sensory organs produce any knowledge. At the heart of these questions is Aristotle's epistemology and especially his notion of the acquisition of knowledge. One of his most powerful assertions

---

4. Groarke, *Aristotelian Account of Induction*, 10.
5. Groarke, *Aristotelian Account of Induction*, 326.
6. Bäck, "Aristotle's Discovery of First Principles," 166.
7. Groarke, *Aristotelian Account of Induction*, 160.

A Brief Survey of the Scholarship on Aristotle's First Principles

of the procurement of knowledge comes from the *Metaphysics*, where he states:

> All men naturally desire knowledge. An indication of this is our esteem for the senses; for apart from their use we esteem them for their own sake, and most of all the sense of sight. Not only with a view to action, but even when no action is contemplated, we prefer sight, generally speaking, to all other senses. The reason of this is that of all the senses sight best helps us to know things, and reveals many distinctions.[8]

Aristotle's concept of knowledge here is twofold: it is not only perceptual knowledge but also knowledge to understand.[9] It is also important to note "knowing in the sense of 'perceiving' is the foundation of 'knowing' in the sense of understanding."[10] Aristotle puts a high epistemic value on perception in understanding the world and the peculiarities of it.

As an empiricist and observationist, Aristotle contends that knowledge is neither inherited from birth nor derived from innate ideas, internal stimuli, or higher states of knowledge. He avows that there is no intellectual cognition or imprint of knowledge inherent in the mind, rather the mind starts from scratch like a blank slate waiting to be written on by sense perception and experience. What we know about animals, sizes, and shapes, etc., is after the fact or posteriori knowledge. It is Aristotle's conviction that induction is how we engage, interact, and know objects of perception either "directly or indirectly."[11]

In *On the Soul*, Aristotle maintains that sight is to color, hearing is of sound, and taste is of flavor.[12] These sensory organs have the ability to discriminate one object from another, such as "the eye discriminates red from green, the common sense between a

---

8. Aristotle, *Metaph*. 980a 1.

9. Leroi, *Lagoon*, 40.

10. Leroi, *Lagoon*, 40.

11. Bäck, *Aristotle's Theory of Abstraction*, 12. See Aristotle, *Eth Nic*. 1139b27–31.

12. Aristotle, *De an* 2.6.

Appendix

color and a flavor."[13] The unique nature of sensory organs grants the subject the ability to know what a thing entails. Aristotle maintains, however, since knowledge emanates from sensation, if there is a defect of any particular sensory organ, such as blindness, there is also a defect or absence in optical knowledge, and if there is a loss of hearing, there is also a loss in auditory knowledge.[14] Aristotle would thus argue that perceptible knowledge (a priori knowledge) of colors, shapes, and sizes is inaccessible unless they are under the rubric of empiricism.

In his perceptible theory, Aristotle contends that sensible objects are threefold in nature: special (or proper), incidental (or accidental) and common.[15] Special and common sensibles are perceived directly. Special sensibles such as colors, sounds, and smells are perceived by one sense while common sensibles such as movement, number, shape, and size are perceived by several senses. Incidental sensibles involve a combination of two or more sensibles that are accidents such as the perception of the color of a particular object. In addition, the dispositions of sensible objects are inherent in potentiality and not in actuality. Sensible objects remain in potentiality before the perceiver perceives the object.[16] For actual sensation to occur or to perceive in actuality, one must be subject to some external object; that is, the perceiver must perceive and have an interaction with the perceptible object.

Aristotle states "that what is placed on the sense organ should be imperceptible is common to all senses; but to perceive no smell without inhaling seems to be peculiar to man."[17] The crucial point in special sensibles is that "each sense has its proper sphere, nor is it deceived as to the fact colour or sound, but only as to the nature and position of the coloured object or the thing which makes the sound."[18] If I see the color red or a red object, that is actually what I

13. Ramírez, "Aristotle on Perception and Universals," 6.
14. Aristotle, *An. post.* 1.18.
15. Aristotle, *De an* 2.6.
16. Aristotle, *De an* 5.4.
17. Aristotle, *De an* 2.9.
18. Aristotle, *De an* 2.6.

see. In special sensibles, Aristotle's theory holds true under normal conditions, but if there are aberrations in perception such as optical illusion or drunkenness the perceptible object is predisposed to variations by the perceiver.[19]

Aristotle concludes that common sensibles are endowed with certain properties, "but perception of movement, rest, number, shape and size is shared by several senses. For things of this kind are not proper to any one sense, but are common to all; for instance, some kinds of movement are perceptible both by touch and by sight."[20] The peculiarity of common sensibles or objects is that they are not confined to one sense, because other sensibles participate in sensory recognition. One can both perceive a car in motion and hear the motion of a turbocharged engine. One can perceive the size of turbocharged sports car as well as the tactile shape of its body.

However, "the senses are liable to error in dealing with the common sensibles but they are not mistaken about the objects of the specific senses, for instance sight is not in error about colours, nor hearing about sound."[21] An inquisitive mind may wonder why, if both special and common sensibles are engaged optically with a perceptible object, they would yield different truths when one is in error and the other is not under normal circumstances. Irving Block answers this question:

> If the common sensibles are directly perceived, why are they not always true in normal perception as are the specific sensibles? The answer is that the individual senses which happen to perceive the common sensibles were not designed specifically to perceive these common sensibles. True, sight perceives shape as directly as it perceives colour, but it does so as a sort of "by-product." It perceives shape because it perceives colour, or its perception of shape is dependent upon its perception of colour. So likewise with the other individual senses. They perceive the common sensibles but the structures or natures

---

19. Aristotle, *Metaph.* 4.5.23.
20. Aristotle, *De an* 2.6.
21. Block, "Truth and Error," 5–6.

Appendix

of the individual senses were not fitted to perceive the common sensibles. They were not "cut-out" for this type of work and therefore, even when functioning normally, they can be mistaken about them. A sign of this is that none of the common sensibles is restricted to one individual sense alone. Therefore, none of the individual senses could have been fashioned specifically to perceive any of the common sensibles, for if this were the case, only one individual sense and no other would perceive a common sensible as we find with the specific sensibles.[22]

The fallibility is not in the special sensibles that are designed for one specific purpose but rather when these particular sensibles interact with the common sensibles, this leads to the possibility of error.

Concerning incidental sensibles, Aristotle explains that "the senses perceive each other's proper objects incidentally, not in their own identity, but acting together as one, when sensation occurs simultaneously in the case of the same object, as for instance of bile, that is bitter and yellow."[23] If I behold a particular red apple (which is incidental in itself) and that the apple also happens to be juicy is incidental. Incidental sensibles are oriented to particular objects such as man; one may perceive more than just a man but Plato incidentally is a man. What marks an object incidental is the color observed through special and common sensibles. Incidental sensibles are not segregated from special and common sensibles; in fact, they are reliant on and work simultaneously with special and common sensibles.

It is not surprising to learn the incongruity that exists among scholars of the peculiarities of Aristotle's explanation of the qualities of sensibles, and two views are of note; the sense datum and material object views. The sense datum view holds that "when one perceives white, what one sees is some bit of white that cannot properly be said to be a white something or other. One does not perceive a white horse directly, but something along the lines of

---

22. Block, "Truth and Error," 6.
23. Aristotle, *De an* 3.2.

an undifferentiated white shape."²⁴ The material object interpretation states that "it is the natural and primary function of an eye to perceive its proper sensible, e.g., the colour white, accurately. However, when the eye sees white, it actually sees the true colour of the object."²⁵ The difference between these two physiologies is that the material objects view contends both object and color go hand in hand, when one perceives the object, one also perceives the color.²⁶ The sense datum view contends that what a person sees is a white shape.²⁷ Although Madden believes material object analysis is consistent with Aristotle's teleology, he also finds textual support for this position in Aristotle's *Metaphysics*. He concludes:

> What is primary metaphysically is also primary in account; since individual substances are the ontological presupposition of sensible qualities our understanding of the latter is parasitic upon our understanding of the former. Thus, Aristotle would then be equally suspicious of any claim to one's having perceived the sensible quality white without having also perceived is as the white sense object. Furthermore, it makes no sense from an Aristotelian point of view for one to claim to have universal knowledge of white without also having perceived white particulars. There just is no such thing in an Aristotelian universal as a quality in isolation from the object in which it is instantiated.²⁸

Block also asserts:

> Aristotle might have argued, Nature made everything for a purpose, and the purpose of man is to understand Nature through science. Thus it would have been a contradiction for Nature to have fashioned man and his organs in such a way that all knowledge and science must, from its inception, be false. For if the foundation and

---

24. Madden, "Aristotle, Induction, and First Principles," 47.
25. Madden, "Aristotle, Induction, and First Principles," 47.
26. Madden, "Aristotle, Induction, and First Principles," 46–48.
27. Madden, "Aristotle, Induction, and First Principles," 46–47.
28. Madden, "Aristotle, Induction, and First Principles," 49–50.

Appendix

beginning of all science, which is perception, be untrue, then all knowledge based on it must be misled.[29]

One of the ways scientists discovered that icebergs were melting in Antarctica was empirically through perceptible (photo) images and constant observation of changing sea levels, this perceptibility inform scientists about the nature of things. I agree with Block and Madden that the material object analysis stresses Aristotle's perceptible theory more than the sense datum view. The material object analysis holds that the senses have a teleological intent designed to portray nature exactly as intended. Thus, "if the foundation and beginning of all science, which is perception, be untrue, then all knowledge based on it must be untrue, then all knowledge based on it must be misled."[30] One can imagine the residual effect it would have on epistemology if perception of sensible objects were always in flux because of its unpredictable nature. There is an element of abstruseness that is incidental to the ontology of perception and that does not repudiate the idea perception is the capacity with which we are endowed to perceive perceptible objects. Perception is how we form beliefs, opinions, theories, and become aware of the existence of things. Aristotle holds that under normal conditions special sensibles are true despite some person's inability to access them the same way. If two men without sensory defect are looking at the same white object both would conclude that the object is white.

To the last point. Well known is Aristotle's belief that physical objects do not exist without form and matter, because both form and matter are necessary elements in things that exist. Matter is not of great import here because it is the perceptible form that we perceive and not the matter. The actual perception of a sensible object form and matter are divorced from each other. In other words, "when the mind perceives a stone, it receives the appearances of the stone: the material mineral that is the stone is left outside, but the shape, size, colour, texture, etc., enters into the mind. We are

29. Block, "Truth and Error," 8–9.
30. Block, "Truth and Error," 9.

A Brief Survey of the Scholarship on Aristotle's First Principles

left with an intellectual copy minus the original matter, as the copy takes up residence in the mind."[31] If a person perceives a green cucumber, what actually occurs is that the person receives the form of the cucumber without the matter.

Observation

Many of Aristotle's theories and judgments were predicated on empirical observation; no subject was out of reach of empirical investigation. They encompass the behavior and biology of animal and aquatic life, botany, physics, natural philosophy, and zoology, etc. It is surprising that "Aristotle never called himself a 'scientist,' . . . he did have a term for 'natural science'—*physike* episteme, literally the 'study of nature.' And he called himself not merely a *physiologos*—'one who gives an account of nature'—but a *physikos*—'one who understands nature.'"[32] Although Aristotle did not have the benefit of advanced technology to investigate the nature of things, he is still considered by some to be "the greatest ancient commentator on animal anatomy and behavior, [who] believed in the importance of direct observation, and some of his comments have been vindicated in modern times."[33] He surely dedicated an enormous amount of time to observational analysis, by examining the activity of living beings, collecting and abstracting, formulating and verifying his theses. Hanne Andersen and Brian Hepburn state:

> In the *Prior* and *Posterior Analytics*, Aristotle reflects first on the aims and then the methods of inquiry into nature. A number of features can be found which are still considered by most to be essential to science. For Aristotle, empiricism, careful observation (but passive observation, not controlled experiment), is the starting point, though the aim is not merely recording of facts. Science (*epistêmê*), for Aristotle, is a body of properly arranged knowledge or

---

31. Groarke, *Aristotelian Account of Induction*, 339.
32. Leroi, *Lagoon*, 40.
33. Hughes, *Pan's Travail*, 108.

Appendix

learning—the empirical facts, but also their ordering and display are of crucial importance. The aims of discovery, ordering, and display of facts partly determine the methods required of successful scientific inquiry.[34]

Aristotle concerns himself with systemization and the causes of the nature of things. In one particular observation he states that "the antelopes and the gazelles, which, although they withstand some attackers and defend themselves with their horns, run away from really fierce fighters."[35] He further explains:

> If one wanted to know whether fish sleep, one would first observe fish in their environment. If one of the behaviors of the fish meets the common understanding of sleep (such as being deadened to outside stimulus, showing little to no movement, and so forth), then one may move to the generalization that fish sleep. But one cannot stop there. Once one has determined that fish sleep (via the inductive mode of discovery), it is now up to the researcher to ferret out the causes and reasons why, in a systematic fashion.[36]

This inductive process Aristotle applies to fish involves a movement that is developed through repeated observation of particular objects. It is through observation and research that he determined the biology of fish, and that a fish releases water out of its mouth after taking it in. Although there is much more to be said, the point I wish to make is Aristotle forms many generalizations and universal conclusion based on empirical observation.

Particular Objects

A particular object is something that exist separately from other things such as a rock from a tree, a horse from a dog, and a banana from an apple. The particular object is identifiable by possessing

---

34. Hepburn and Andersen, "Scientific Method."
35. Aristotle, *Part. an.* 3.2.
36. Boylan, "Aristotle," 44–77. See Aristotle, *On Sleeping and Waking* 455b 8, cf. Aristotle, *On Dreams* 458b 9.

A Brief Survey of the Scholarship on Aristotle's First Principles

certain qualities and properties, thus each particular perceptual object in a given sphere is determined by what makes a thing what it is. Although no universal predication or definition can explain one particular object, knowledge can still be ascertained. Aristotle states that the senses do not tell us the why of anything, such as, why fire is hot; they can only say that it is hot.[37] One learns by touching that same hot object again will burn, producing knowledge, or the fact that one can distinguish two colors such as green and not red is a form of knowledge.

Particulars and Universals

What relationship does the first particular has to other particulars of the same class? Aristotle answerers this question by stating, "If we could see the channels of the burning glass and the light passing through, it would also be obvious why it burns; because we should see the effect severally in each particular instance, and appreciate at the same time that this is what happens in every case."[38] It is not that an individual instance of perceiving the burning glass that harvests universal knowledge, it only does if we can piece together more cases (particulars) to explain why it burns.[39] Aristotle answers the question again by offering the astronomy behind an eclipse, "If we were on the moon[,] we should not be inquiring either as to the fact or the reason, but both fact and reason would be obvious simultaneously. For the act of perception would have enabled us to know the universal too; since, the present fact of an eclipse being evident, perception would then at the same time give us the present fact of the [earth's] screening the sun's light, and from this would arise the universal."[40] Peter Adamson points out that this illustration of an eclipse is surely "designed to deal with questions that are, in the first instance, about particulars

---

37. Aristotle, *Metaph.* 1.1.13.
38. Aristotle, *An. post.* 1.31.
39. Ramirez, "Aristotle on Perception and Universals," 60.
40. Aristotle, *An. post.* 2.2.

Appendix

('why is this eclipse happening?'). We explain a particular eclipse by subsuming it under an explanation of eclipses in general."[41] I would add Aristotle could have developed his theory of how an eclipse occurs through previous research, but his understanding of this phenomenon likely occurred through repeated observations of individual eclipses.[42] Ramirez concludes:

> Similarly, we should say that, in actuality, perception is of particulars and not of universals (e.g., when I see a blue book I do not see the set of all blue things or the set of all books). This is the sense used in *Post. An.* I.31. However, in potentiality, perception is of universals. I am *able* to perceive all blue things and, since universals are classes, I am able to perceive the universal blue. Furthermore, when I perceive a blue book, what I perceive is *per accidens* a blue thing, i.e., a member of the universal BLUE. This is the sense of *Post. An.* II.19. If this is so, then there is no inconsistency in saying that perception is (actually) of particulars and (potentially and *per accidens*) of universals.[43]

Hence, universals are predicated and constructed on the ontology of particular objects. If redness exists in universals the color red must exist somehow in (a given) particular object. Wingate asserts that, "indeed, at the perceptual stage an inquiring subject may not even have the concepts necessary to articulate what she perceives, much less reason about it. Still, the perceiving subject will bear some relation to the universals instantiated by the things she perceives—and this, together with the subject's other cognitive capacities, will allow her to develop a more advanced grasp of universals."[44] If it holds that a coherent and systematic relationship of universals are grounded in particular objects, and that particular objects are inherent in sensory perception, it is natural

---

41. Adamson, "On Knowledge of Particulars," 260.

42. Aristotle, *An. post.* 2.2. Aristotle also states, "The fact that the eclipse was now taking place would be obvious, and sense perception would tell us that the earth was now obstructing the light, from this the universal would follow."

43. Ramirez, "Aristotle on Perception and Universals," 62.

44. Wingate, "Aristotle on Induction and First Principles," 16.

A Brief Survey of the Scholarship on Aristotle's First Principles

to reason that concepts must have their origins in the perceiver's actualization of the perceptible object. If "someone who believes that concepts—those defined in an Aristotelian science, for example—are gained by experience should believe that in perception, conceptual elements are present in some way."[45] When we perceive the moon, we are not absent of recognition; we naturally realize its shape is circular and that it is the moon.

Aristotle explains man is a universal, Callias a particular. He contends that once we know man and not just the man Callias, we can define universal properties that belong to man. To understand that man is a rational animal separate and distinct from irrational animals, a myriad of men must be in view, not one. An individual man might possess qualities that are not commensurate in the universal man such as different personality traits or even a lost body part, but such differences do not disqualify him as being human. It is not what we know about a particular dog that yields universals, but rather what we discovered in all dogs, such as, all dogs have a sense of smell, or all dogs wag their tails to communicate meaning.

Memory

Aristotle differentiates between what memory is and what it is not. He states, "But memory is of the past; no one could claim to remember the present while it is present. For instance one cannot remember a particular white object while one is looking at it, nor can one remember a subject of theoretical speculation while one is actually speculating and thinking about it."[46] In other words, when the current sensible experience is no longer actively present in the mind or calculatedly being thought of, or one is no longer engaged in the experience, then it becomes memory. This time-based

---

45. King, *Aristotle and Plotinus on Memory*, 5.
46. Aristotle, *Mem. rem.* 449b. He also explains, "Memory, then, is neither sensation nor judgment, but is a state or affection of one these, when time has elapsed. There can be no memory of something now present at the present time, as has been said, but sensation refers to what is present, expectation to what is future, and memory to what is past. All memory, then, implies lapse of time."

Appendix

marker can be explained by "three forms of cognition, all directed at objects characterised by their own modus of time: perception is of the present, expectation of the future and memory of the past. Each is distinguished from the others by the temporal status of its objects."[47] Thus, "the original experience and the moment of the memory" are not simultaneous.

In Aristotle's *Metaphysics*, he discloses the cumulative effect of multiple experiences and how these memory facts generate universals. In a rather lengthy but important illustration, he states:

> It is from memory that men acquire experience, because the numerous memories of the same thing eventually produce the effect of a single experience. Experience seems very similar to science and art, but actually it is through experience that men acquire science and art; for as Polus rightly says, "experience produces art, but inexperience chance." Art is produced when from many notions of experience a single universal judgment is formed with regard to like objects. To have a judgment that when Callias was suffering from this or that disease this or that benefited him, and similarly with Socrates and various other individuals, is a matter of experience; but to judge that it benefits all persons of a certain type, considered as a class, who suffers from this or that disease (e.g. the phlegmatic or bilious when suffering from burning fever) is a matter of art. [He further explains that] It would seem that for practical purposes experience is in no respect inferior to art; indeed we see men of experience succeeding more than those who have theory without experience. The reason of this is that experience is knowledge of particulars, but art of universals; and actions and the effects produced are all concerned with the particular. For it is not man that the physician cures, except incidentally, but Callias or Socrates or some other person similarly named, who is incidentally a man as well. So if a man has theory without experience, and knows the universal, but does not know the particular contained in it, he will often fail in his treatment; for it

---

47. King, *Aristotle and Plotinus on Memory*, 27–28.

is the particular that must be treated. Nevertheless we consider that knowledge and proficiency belong to art rather than experience, and we assume that artists are wiser than men of mere experience (which implies that in all cases wisdom depends rather upon knowledge); and this is because the former know the cause, whereas the latter do not. For the experienced know the fact, but not the wherefore; but the artists know the wherefore and the cause.[48]

In Aristotle's hierarchal order, we perceive, remember, experience, and consequently, we advance in knowledge about certain objects, and the arts and sciences are actuated from there. Aristotle also tells us that "several memories of the same thing produce finally the capacity for a single experience." He implies that one object (of the same kind, not several) supplies several memories or facts about a thing.[49] The phrase "same thing" could be interpreted as different facets of the same object. If a person perceives a particular table by looking at it on different occasions over time, the person accumulates stored memory facts of the perceptible act in his or her soul.[50]

Several memories of different things do not constitute a single experience. In other words, two different experiences from unrelated domain experiences will yield two different memory facts.

Recollection

Any discussion of Aristotle's memory is inevitably a discussion that encompasses recollection. The psychology to recollect is not trivial especially since Aristotle devoted an entire chapter to it in his treatise *On Memory and Recollection*. In his explanation

48. Aristotle, *Metaph.* 1.1.4–11.

49. He also states that "where perception does persist, after the act of perception is over the percipients can still retain the perception in the soul. If this happens repeatedly, a distinction immediately arises between those animals which derive a coherent impression from the persistence and those which do not." *An. post.* 2.14.

50. Gregorić and Grgić, "Aristotle's Notion of Experience," 14.

Appendix

of memory and recollection, Aristotle states, "For recollection is neither the recovery nor the acquisition of memory; for when one first learns or receives a sense impression, one does not recover any memory (for none has gone before), nor does one acquire it for the first time; it is only at the moment when the state or affection has been induced that there is memory."[51] It is of note, the original perception or image that is sought remains dormant or inactive until there is an attempt to recollect it through an initial search. This attempt requires an active search of the image (object or subject) under change. If a person wishes to recollect an experience of the past say, a particular traumatic experience that presently evades the person's mind; that experience begins with a search.

If one remembers a perception without a search, however, this suggests there is an aspect of memory that is not contingent on recollection. One may know or remember past objects and subjects spontaneously or involuntarily without much determination. For instance, "Socrates can say he remembers Theaetetus without a search."[52] If we "ask Socrates what he is doing when he is doing geometry he would answer that he is doing geometry: not I am remembering these geometrical figures."[53] Knowing at the moment is not the same as actively searching for past perceptions. In addition, sometimes we can actively search for a past image without success, but by fortuity or through some other capacity the impression comes to mind. If "I wish to remember Cebes' face[,] I try to recollect but fail. Sometime later, while I still have the wish to remember what Cebes looks like, but am not currently trying to do it, I see Simmias, and because I have seen the two together so often, I immediately recall Cebes' features."[54] Sorabji explains, "The recovery of perception will involve not perceiving again, but having an image of what was perceived."[55] The original perceptible experience is not what remains in the soul but the image.

51. Aristotle, *Mem. rem* 1–2.
52. King, *Aristotle and Plotinus on Memory*, 94.
53. King, *Aristotle and Plotinus on Memory*, 30.
54. King, *Aristotle and Plotinus on Memory*, 100–101.
55. Sorabji, *Aristotle on Memory*, 92.

A Brief Survey of the Scholarship on Aristotle's First Principles

These objects of perception or experiences that one recollects characteristically occur through what Aristotle calls "laws of association." The thought of one idea stimulates another idea or object that resembles another, until the thing sought is discovered. If one thinks of an apple, he will associate the apple with fruit or when a person sees dark clouds, he will associate that for the most part with rain. When we hunt for the next in a series implies an active and deliberate search (and perhaps unsuccessful) of past perceptual experiences that are already stored in the memory. It is not only one perceptual image that takes place in the process of recollection, but the case may be that "when we recollect, then, we re-experience one of our former impulses, until at last we experience that which customarily precedes the one which we require."[56] This search includes what is similar or contrary or contiguous to the thing we seek. Suffice it to say that the objects of memory can be abstracted through similar ideas, colors, patterns, locations or shared properties and relationships. For something contiguous, if a person "wants to recollect what he did last Tuesday, he starts with what he did last Monday, which is neighboring. By this means, with any luck, he will be led straight from his starting—point to the thing he is seeking, and so he will have taken a shortcut."[57] Reliving the events on Monday actuates the events on Tuesday. Perhaps the most important aspect of memory that concerns us here is not the capacity for memory and recollection but more so how knowledge is made assessable through memory and recollection.

Experience

Aristotle's theory of perception and sensory organs are innately connected to memory. On the one hand, the percept or object are stored in memory retrievable through a search, on the other, memory provides stored facts of past experiences that inevitably

---

56. Aristotle, *Mem. rem*, 2.
57. Sorabji, *Aristotle on Memory*, 43–44.

Appendix

allows a person to make knowledge claims.[58] His notion of "experience fills a wide gap between the non-rational cognitive capacities of perception and memory on the one side, and the rational cognitive dispositions of art and science on the other side."[59] On the face of it, art and science are cognitive and relational to the non rational capacity of perception and memory.

Now as we probe into what Aristotle calls experience and the nuances of it, the ontology of experience is that each percept or experience makes a stand or comes to a halt in the soul. He states that "when a retreat has occurred in battle, if one man halts so does another, and then another, until the original position is restored. The soul is so constituted that it is capable of the same sort of process."[60] Aristotle reiterates:

> Let us restate what we said just now with insufficient precision. As soon as one individual percept has "come to a halt" in the soul, this is the first beginning of the presence there of a universal (because although it is the particular that we perceive, the act of perception involves the universal, e.g., "man," not "a man, Callias"). Then other "halts" occur among these < proximate> universals, until the indivisible genera or < ultimate> universals are established. E.g., a particular species of animal leads to the genus "animal," and so on.[61]

In Aristotle's battle illustration, the stimulus behind these stands are congruent with the next stand. The development of a first universal in the soul form the next stand. Thus each stand is progressive which builds upon the memory, thoughts, and ideas of previous stands or experiences. Once a person's experience grows, the explanation also grows.

Let us look at another point. If we examine again the illustration mentioned above of Callias and Socrates, a distinction can be made between a person who has experience, but not the art and

---

58. Gregorić and Grgić, "Aristotle's Notion of Experience," 14.
59. Gregorić and Grgić, "Aristotle's Notion of Experience," 2.
60. Aristotle, *An. post.* 2.19.
61. Aristotle, *An. post.* 2.19.

skill in a given domain. We should point out that although the person may not possess the art and skill in a given domain that does not preclude the person from explicating propositions and recognizing certain principles and facts in a given domain. Surely experience is essential to art and skill in which it is impossible to bring about scientific knowledge without it; thus both experience and art/skill are mutually dependent on the other. Aristotle states, "Science and art come to men through experience; for experience made art as Polus says, but inexperience luck." If art is induced without experience, it is by chance, but if art is logically imparted from experience, "it follows that experience must somehow provide all the relevant explanatory items, including the principles of art and science."[62] An electrical apprentice gains experience before he or she is considered a skilled trade's person, and a person trained and experienced in dental health is not oblivious to certain principles of oral health, i.e., gingivitis, dental radiology, and preventive care. Knowing the individual case of Callias, who suffered from a particular illness, the general practitioner recognized that what cured him would also cure Socrates because they had similar medical dispositions.

Aristotle would claim, however, regardless of how much experience a person has in a particular domain, and how experience contributes to art and science, his or her knowledge will always be restricted, because that person lacks the ability to explain why something is the case. Even though dental hygienists are trained in dentistry and able to provide general knowledge about it, their field of study or skills are not equivalent to the dentist, who is able to diagnose and provide specific knowledge about dentistry, i.e., teeth, gums, and hygiene. Having experience alone will always be limited in scope in a specific domain, particularly if a person is unable to explain the causation behind the scientific theory. Wingate explains that "a physician possessing the craft of medicine differs from an experienced doctor in two significant ways: first, the physician can identify the explanation for some successful treatment, while the experienced doctor acts without any explanatory

---

62. Gregorić and Grgić, "Aristotle's Notion of Experience," 21.

Appendix

knowledge, and second, the physician can recognize the effects of some type of disease in some type of patient, while the experienced doctor merely treats symptoms on a particular, case-by-case basis."[63] Thus, the distinction is that the physician possesses explanatory power and knows the causes, while the experienced doctor is limited in his explanation and is unable to explain the cause. Experience merely enables a person to proceed to a certain point in scientific understanding, but the person will inevitably fall short of grasping the cause and nature which the domain requires.

A Brief Survey on Nous

Aristotle's theory of nous is multifaceted, which makes it difficult to deal with his theory substantially. It is impossible nevertheless to sufficiently elucidate Aristotle's induction and universals without stating a few things about his concept of nous. In *Posterior Analytics*, Aristotle explains one of the functions of nous:

> Now of the intellectual faculties that we use in the pursuit of truth some (e.g., scientific knowledge and intuition) are always true, whereas others (e.g., opinion and calculation) admit falsity; and no other kind of knowledge except intuition is more accurate than scientific knowledge. Also first principles are more knowable than demonstration, and all scientific knowledge involves reason. It follows that there can be no scientific knowledge of the first principles; and since nothing can be more infallible than scientific knowledge except intuition, it must be intuition that apprehends first principles. . . . Therefore, since we possess no other infallible faculty besides scientific knowledge, the source from which such knowledge starts must be intuition. Thus it will be the primary source of scientific knowledge that apprehends the first principles, while scientific knowledge as a whole is similarly related to the world of facts.[64]

---

63. Wingate, "Aristotle on Induction and First Principles," 17.
64. Aristotle, *An. post.* 2.19.

A Brief Survey of the Scholarship on Aristotle's First Principles

Aristotle clearly puts the onus of discovery of first principles on nous. But if nous is responsible for acquiring first principles, how can induction likewise yield these same principles.[65] In fact, a person who investigates these matters may even conclude why induction is necessary because first principles can be ascertained through nous.[66]

Aristotle explains the importance of induction in the process of discovery. He contends that "it is impossible to gain scientific knowledge of them [first principles], since they can neither be apprehended from universals without induction."[67] He also concludes that "a particular species of animal leads to the genus 'animal,' and so on. Clearly then it must be by induction that we acquire knowledge of the primary premises, because this is also the way in which general concepts are conveyed to us by sense perception."[68] Aristotle recognizes the importance of induction and the responsibility this method has for acquiring scientific knowledge, but this recognition does not resolve the critical inquiry of how to discriminate, and describe the relationship between the two concepts, that is, induction and nous. James H. Lesher provides us with an explanation:

> The relation between νοῦς and ἐπαγωγή turns out to be a typically Aristotelian one: there is one activity, grasping the universal principle, but it admits of various descriptions; to speak of it as an act of νόησις is to give an epistemological characterization, while to characterize it as ἐπαγωγή is to speak of methodology. This account of νοῦς and ἐπαγωγή coincides with Aristotle's view that experience provides us with principles which we then endeavor to structure within syllogistic form, and it makes perfectly good sense of νοῦς as the "source of scientific knowledge" since it is νοῦς which supplies us in general with such principles.[69]

---

65. Murat, "Aristotle on Episteme and Nous," 4–5.
66. Lesher, "Meaning of ΝΟΥΣ," 44–45.
67. Aristotle, *An. post.* 1.18.
68. Aristotle, *An. post.* 2.19.
69. Lesher, *Meaning of* ΝΟΥΣ, 58.

Appendix

Thus induction is primarily the method by way of experience that assist in understanding scientific principles, and nous is the intellectual capacity to comprehend what we experience. John Arthos also explains: "All matters of conduct belong to the class of particular and ultimate things that they are starting points. They are grasped by intelligence or intuition (nous) in a way similar to the immutable and primary definitions in formal logic. . . . The intuition of the particular starting point, the ultimate particular, does not relieve us of the obligation to reason inductively, but rather makes it possible."[70] It is not that nous postpones comprehension until the inductive process is over to validate the experience; nous contributes throughout the inductive process to confirm the theory in the initial and final stages of acquiring the epistemology of a thing. Even in perception, nous subtly or invariably takes place.

The fact that induction is incapable of securing scientific knowledge alone, does not deny that it participates in achieving those ends. Both induction and nous have a similar disposition epistemically, the latter more forceful than the former. Even though nous provides the insight that bridges the gap between particulars and universals, Pedersen reminds us that "*nous* is not a faculty that guarantees the truth of a universal proposition that is grasped on the basis of inspection of particular cases, it is only a faculty that makes possible that grasp, whether the result be true or false."[71] Because perception and experience are unable to achieve universals alone, another capacity enables a person to grasp them, namely nous.

Aristotle's Universals

Aristotle's universals systematically move from perception through the process of induction to particular objects of a certain class say, a bird (species), along with the intellectual capacity of nous to an observation of qualities and behaviors about several birds of that

---

70. Arthos, "Where There Are No Rules," 325. See NE, VI, xi, 3–4.
71. Pedersen, "More on Aristotelian Epagoge," 311.

A Brief Survey of the Scholarship on Aristotle's First Principles

class. We infer from there to universals (genus) and definitions and explanations of the causes of the thing.[72] This is the general sequence of reaching universals in Aristotle's system of thought.

As we delve into Aristotle universals, it is essential to state first that he believes in the physical existence of things in the world, and that "there are no universals that are unattached to existing things. . . . If a universal exists either as a particular or a relation, then there must have been, must be currently, or must be in the future, something on which the universal can be predicated."[73] In this sense universal concepts already exist in living species before universals are discovered in particular (objects). In addition, "if Aristotle holds universals to be abstracted from sense perceptions, he has to be admitting that the universals are contained somehow already in the sense perception."[74] We may take this a step further and say a particular sensible object may contain universals before the actuality of sense perception.

The focal point of Aristotle's universals, however, is his theory of forms and substances. Aristotle's predecessor and mentor was Plato, who contends that reality is identifiable in forms or ideas such as dog, cat, beauty, justice, or courage. Plato's philosophy on the form of beauty is relegated to the senses (such as what we may find in a person or in art) but also to the abstract. He contends we have our own conceptual understanding of what beauty is in the natural realm, but there is also an otherworldly beauty that exists in the abstract, where perfection is. Moreover, "Plato maintained that particular things continually change in so far as things may deform or degrade and, thus, are unreliable to our senses. It is the universal Form of these physical objects that offers reliability."[75] Needless to say, Aristotle objects to Plato's idea of forms and

---

72. Aristotle points out that "the most universal concepts are furthest from our perception, and particulars are nearest to it; and these are opposite to one another." *An. post.* 1.2.

73. "Aristotle," *New World Encyclopedia*, http://www.Newworldencyclopedia.org/p/index.php?title=Aristtole&oldid=1001625.

74. Bäck, *Aristotle's Theory of Abstraction*, 85.

75. Vezina, "Universals and Particulars," 103.

Appendix

universals. Aristotle asserts that a form of knowledge begins not in the abstract but through sense perception or this worldliness. Two points can be made here: "First, he [Aristotle] argues that Forms cannot constitute a substance; and, secondly, that since Forms are not substances, Forms cannot cause a substance's coming into being."[76] Aristotle's concept of beauty is not identifiable in abstract terms or detached from the natural world, but rather is found in the universal nature of beauty.

The concept of beauty is not an otherworldly idea derived from the realm of perfect forms; instead, we discover the concept of beauty in space and time by individual or particular instances through perception. Vezina contends, "Aristotle argues that reality is not dependent on universal abstracts (Forms), but on particular substances of physical things. As such, Aristotle holds that we can ground our beliefs in the sensible world with some assurance."[77] Truth is therefore obtainable in the natural world.

The Ability to Explain Universals

The distinctive nature of scientific knowledge is that a person not only know certain facts, but also able to explain the cause, while a person who has experience relies on facts. So knowing the facts of a thing is not equivalent to knowing its cause. One has to move from seeking facts to seeking causes and explanations and principles in that domain.[78] The principles in a given domain such as: a physicist's domain is physics, an ecologist's domain is ecology, a theologian's domain is theology, and a musician's domain is music.[79] Aristotle believes that "a science is one if it is concerned

---

76. Vezina, "Universals and Particulars," 101.

77. Vezina, "Universals and Particulars," 101.

78. Gregorić and Grgić, "Aristotle's Notion of Experience," 30–31.

79. Aristotle makes the point that "most of the principles, however, which are connected with a particular science are peculiar to it. I mean, e.g., that is for astronomical experience to convey to us the principles of astronomy (for it was not until the phenomena had been thoroughly apprehended that the demonstrations of astronomy were discovered); and the same applies to any

A Brief Survey of the Scholarship on Aristotle's First Principles

with a single genus or class of objects which are composed of the primary elements of that genus and are parts of it or essential modifications of those parts."[80] Thus, a person who is an expert or specialist in a given domain has explored the idiosyncrasies and scrutinized the nuances of that domain and therefore possesses demonstrable knowledge. It is not enough to have rudimentary skills and basic knowledge because that does not qualify as technē or knowing the principles of a given domain. One may correctly form generalizations and draw true conclusions in a particular domain and yet may be unable to go beyond these generalities. The ability to explain the causes of things one has grasped the principles and scientific understanding of that particular domain. Wingate provides a medical illustration:

> So an experienced doctor would (qua experienced) know only how to deal with the patients and symptoms in front of her, at some determinate time and place—experience is a particular state. . . . Someone with craft-knowledge of medicine, by contrast, would be able to reason (i.e. engage in logos-involving thought) about types of patients and treatments without reference to any particular case, and understand the universal causes underlying her practice. She would understand why certain kinds of patients should be treated someway, rather than merely recognizing that some treatment is called for in this or that case. She would thus know universals *universally*.[81]

It is often the case that medical practitioners have to refer their patients to specialists when their health requires further examination.

---

other art." His point is that most principles are peculiar to the domain of a particular science or field of study. Aristotle, *An. pr.* 1.30.

80. Aristotle, *An. post.* 1.28. Aristotle further states, "One science is different from another if their principles do not belong to the same genus, or if the principles of the one are not derived from the principles of the other." He also states, "Thus the master craftsmen are superior in wisdom, not because they can do things, but because they possess a theory and know the causes." Aristotle, *Metaph.* 1.1.12. Albert Einstein not only experienced the effects of gravity but was able to explain the cause behind this gravitational force.

81. Wingate, "Aristotle on the Perception of Universals," 16.

Appendix

Such a practitioner may be able to give a general diagnosis based on individual cases or previous documented studies, but the professional still must refer the patient to a specialist to determine the specific causes. Aristotle contends:

> Art is produced when from many notions of experience a single universal judgment is formed with regard to like objects. To have a judgment that when Callias was suffering from this or that disease this or that benefited him, and similarly with Socrates and various other individuals, is a matter of experience; but to judge that it benefits all persons of a certain type, considered as a class, who suffers from this or that disease (e.g. the phlegmatic or bilious when suffering from burning fever) is a matter of art.[82]

Experience constitutes individualized cases, namely, Callias and Socrates, so they will always be restricted to the domain of experience. Once we have enough experiences, however, and there is a factual relationship that holds true not only among these individual experiences, but also when it benefits all persons of that class. The person then possesses the essence of what a thing is, not in a rudimentary way, but fully grasping its concept and nature. These shared or essential properties and substances that shape the essence of what a thing is.

---

82. Aristotle, *Metaph.* 1.1.5–6.

Bibliography

Adamson, Peter. "On Knowledge of Particulars." *Proceedings of the Aristotelian Society* 105 (2005) 273–94.
Anderson, R. Dean, Jr. *Ancient Rhetorical Theory and Paul*. Rev. ed. Contributions to Biblical Exegesis and Theology 18. Leuven: Peeters, 1999.
———. *Glossary of Greek Rhetorical Terms Connected to Methods of Argumentation, Figures and Tropes from Anaximenes to Quintilian*. Contributions to Biblical Exegesis and Theology 24. Leuven: Peeters, 2000.
Aristotle. *The Art of Rhetoric*. Translated by John Henry Freese. LCL. Cambridge: Harvard University Press, 2006.
———. *Metaphysics I–IX*. Translated by Hugh Tredennick. LCL. Cambridge: Harvard University Press, 1933.
———. *Nicomachean Ethic*. Translated with an introduction and notes by Martin Ostwald. Hoboken, NJ: Prentice Hall, 1999.
———. *On the Soul; Parva Naturalia; On Breath*. Translated by W. S. Hett. Cambridge: Harvard University Press, 1957.
———. *Parts of Animals; Movement of Animals; Progression of Animals*. Translated by A. L. Peck and E. S. Forster. LCL. Cambridge: Harvard University Press, 1937.
———. *Posterior Analytics*. Edited and translated by Hugh Tredennick. LCL. Cambridge: Harvard University Press, 1997.
———. *Prior Analytics*. Translated by Hugh Tredennick. LCL. Cambridge: Harvard University Press, 1967.

Bibliography

———. *Problems 1–38*. Edited and translated by W. S. Hett. LCL. Cambridge: University Press, 2011.

———. *Rhetoric to Alexander*. Edited and translated by David C. Mirhady. LCL. Cambridge: Harvard University Press, 2011.

———. *Topica*. Translated by E. S. Forster. LCL. Cambridge: Harvard University Press, 1997.

Arnold, C. E. "I Am Astonished That You Are So Quickly Turning Away! (Gal 1.6) Paul and Anatolian Folk Belief." *New Testament Studies* 51 (2005) 429–49.

Arthos, John. "Where There Are No Rules or Systems to Guide Us: Argument from Example in a Hermeneutic Rhetoric." *Quarterly Journal of Speech* 89 4 (2003) 320–44.

Ashcraft, Morris. "Paul Defends His Apostleship Galatians 1 and 2." *Review and Expositor* 69 (1972) 459–69.

Aune, David E. *The Westminster Dictionary of New Testament and Early Christian Literature and Rhetoric*. Louisville: Westminster John Knox, 2003.

Bäck, Allan. "Aristotle's Discovery of First Principles." In *From Puzzles to Principles? Essays on Aristotle's Dialectic*, edited by May Sim, 163–81. Lanham, MD: Lexington, 1999.

———. *Aristotle's Theory of Abstraction*. Cham, Switzerland: Springer, 2014.

Bartha, Paul. "Analogy and Analogical Reasoning." In *The Stanford Encyclopedia of Philosophy*, edited by Edward N. Zalta. https://plato.stanford.edu/archives/win2016/entries/reasoning-analogy/>.

Benoit, William. "Aristotle's Example: The Rhetorical Induction." *Quarterly Journal of Speech* 2 (1980) 182–92.

———. "On Aristotle's Example." *Philosophy and Rhetoric* 20 (1987) 261–67.

Blank, Henry Rudolph. "Six Theses concerning Freedom in Christ and Liberation: Liberation in Galatians, Luther, and Liberation Theology." *Concordia Journal* 20 (1994) 236–60.

Block, Irving. "Truth and Error in Aristotle's Theory of Sense Perception." *Philosophical Quarterly* 11 (1961) 1–9.

Blom, Henriette van der. *Cicero's Role Models: The Political Strategy of a Newcomer* Oxford Classical Monographs. New York: Oxford University Press, 2010.

Blount, Brian K. *Revelation: A Commentary*. Louisville: John Knox, 2009.

Blum, Edwin, A. *1 Peter*. In *1, 2 Peter, 1, 2, 3 John, Jude*, by Edwin Blum and Glenn W. Barker. Expositor's Bible Commentary: With the New International Version 12. Grand Rapids: Zondervan, 1981.

Boylan, Michael. "Aristotle: Biology." *Internet Encyclopedia of Philosophy* 19 (1986) 44–77. www.iep.utm.edu/aris-bio.

Brehm, H. Alan. "Paul's Relationship with the Jerusalem Apostles in Galatians 1 and 2." *Scottish Journal of Theology* 37 (1994) 11–16.

Brinton, Alan. "Cicero's Use of Historical Examples in Moral Argument." *Philosophy and Rhetoric* 21 (1988) 169–84.

Bibliography

———. "Galatian Problems: Autobiographical Data." *Bulletin of John Rylands University* (1969) 92–309.
———. *Paul: Apostle of the Heart Set Free*. Grand Rapids: Eerdmans, 1977.
Bruce, F. F. *Paul, Apostle of the Heart Set Free*. Grand Rapids: Eerdmans, 2000.
Burdick, Donald W. *James*. In *Hebrews, James*, by Leon Morris and Donald W. Burdick. Expositor's Bible Commentary: With the New International Version 12. Grand Rapids: Zondervan, 1981.
Burton, DeWitt Ernest. *A Critical and Exegetical Commentary on the Galatians*. International and Critical Commentary. Edinburgh: T. & T. Clark, 1956.
Carson, Donald A. *Matthew*. In *Matthew, Mark, Luke*, by D. A. Carson et al. Expositor's Bible Commentary: With the New International Version of the Holy Bible 8. Edited by Frank E. Gaebelein. Grand Raids: Eerdmans, 1984.
Chaplin, Jane D. *Livy's Exemplary History*. New York: Oxford University Press, 2000.
Cicero. *Rhetorica Ad Herennium*. Translated by Harry Caplan. Edited by Jeffrey Henderson. LCL. Cambridge: Harvard University Press, 2004.
Cosby, Michael R. *The Rhetorical Composition and Function of Hebrews 11: In Light of Example Lists in Antiquity*. Macon: Mercer University, 1988.
De Boer, Martinus C. *Galatians: A Commentary*. Louisville: Westminster, 2011.
deSilva, David A. *Seeing Things John's Way: The Rhetoric of the Book of Revelation*. Grand Rapids: Eerdmans, 2009.
Dodd, Brian. "Christ's Slave, People Pleasers." *New Testament Studies* 42 (1996) 90–104.
Donald, J. *Pan's Travail: Environmental Problems of the Ancient Greeks and Romans*. Baltimore: Johns Hopkins University Press, 1996.
Dunn, J. D. G. "The Incident at Antioch (Gal 2:11–18)." *Journal for the Study of the New Testament* 5 (1983) 3–57.
———. *New Testament Theology: The Theology of Paul's Letter to the Galatians*. Cambridge: Cambridge University Press, 1993.
———."The Relationship between Paul and Jerusalem according to Galatians 1 and 2." *New Testament Studies* 28 (1982) 461–78.
———. *The Theology of Paul the Apostle*. Grand Rapids: Eerdmans, 1998.
Ebeling, Gerhard. *The Truth of the Gospel: An Exposition of Galatians*. Translated by David Green. Philadelphia: Fortress, 1985.
Eggs, Ekkehard, and Dermott McElholm. *Exemplifications, Selections and Argumentations: The Use of Example Markers in English and German*. Frankfurt: Peter Lang, 2013.
Elmer, Ian J. "Setting the Record Straight at Galatia: Paul's Narratio (Gal 1:13—2:14) as Response to the Galatian Conflict." In *Religious Conflict from Early Christianity to the Rise of Islam*, edited by Wendy Mayer and Bronwen Neil, 21–37. Berlin: de Gruyter, 2013.
Engberg-Pedersen, Troels. "The Construction of Religious Experience in Paul." In *Inquiry into Religious Experience in Early Judaism and Early Christianity*, edited by Frances Flannery et al., 147–56. Experientia 1. Atlanta: SBL, 2008.

Bibliography

———. "More on Aristotelian Epagoge." *Phronesis* 24 (1979) 301–19.
Esler, Philip F. "Making and Breaking an Agreement Mediterranean Style: A New Reading of Galatians 2:1–14." *Biblical Interpretation* 3 (1995) 285–314.
Fee, Gordon D. *1 and 2 Timothy, Titus.* New International Biblical Commentary. Peabody, MA: Hendrickson, 1988.
———. *The First Epistle to the Corinthians.* Edited by Ned B. Stonehouse. Grand Rapids: Eerdmans, 1987.
———. *God's Empowering Presence: The Holy Spirit in the Letters of Paul.* Peabody, MA: Hendrickson, 1994.
Fiore, Benjamin. *The Function of Personal Example in Socratic and Pastoral Epistles.* Rome: Biblical Institute, 1986.
Fowl, Stephen E. "Imitation of Paul of Christ." In *Dictionary of Paul and his Letters: A Compendium of Contemporary Biblical Scholarship,* edited by Gerald F. Hawthorne, 428–30. Downers Grove: InterVarsity, 1993.
———. "Who Can Read Abraham's Story? Allegory and Interpretative Power in Galatians." *Journal for the Study of the New Testament* 55 (1994) 77–95.
Fung, Ronald Y. K. *The Epistle to the Galatians.* Grand Rapids: Eerdmans, 1988.
Gale, Herbert M. *The Use of Analogy in the Letters of Paul.* Philadelphia: Westminster, 1964.
Garcia, Eduardo. "Aristotle on Perception and Universals: An Extensional Reading." *Topicos: Revista de Filosofia* 38 (2010) 49–84.
Garland, David E. "Paul's Defense of the Truth of the Gospel Regarding Gentiles (Galatians 2:15—3:22)." *Review and Expositor* 91 (1994) 165–81.
Garver, Eugene. *Aristotle's Rhetoric: An Art of Character.* Chicago: University of Chicago Press, 1994.
Gaventa, Beverly. "Galatians 1 and 2: Autobiography as Paradigm." *Novum Testamentum* 28 (1986) 309–26.
Geldenhuys, Norval. *Commentary on the Gospel of Luke: The English Text with Introduction Exposition and Notes.* Grand Rapids: Eerdmans, 1977.
Gelley, Alexander, ed. *Unruly Examples: On the Rhetoric of Exemplarity.* Stanford: Stanford University Press, 1995.
Gerhardsson, Birger. *Memory and Manuscript: Oral Tradition and Written Transmission in Rabbinic Judaism and Early Christianity with Tradition & Transmission in Early Christianity.* Grand Rapids: Eerdmans, 1998.
Gordon, T. David. "The Problem at Galatia." *Interpretation* 41 (1987) 32–43.
Gregorić, Pavel, and Filip Grgić. "Aristotle's Notion of Experience." *Archiv für Geschichte der Philosophie* 88 (2006) 1–30.
Groarke, Louis. *An Aristotelian Account of Induction: Creating Something from Nothing.* Montreal: McGill, 2009.
———. "Jumping the Gaps: Induction as First Exercise of Intelligence." In *Shifting the Paradigm: Alternative Perspectives on Induction,* edited by Paolo C. Biondi and Louis F. Groarke, 455–514. Berlin: de Gruyter, 2014.
Guthrie, Donald. *Galatians.* New Century Bible. London: Oliphants, 1969.
Hafemann, Scott. "'Noah, the Preacher of (God's) Righteousness': The Argument from Scripture in 2 Peter 2:5 and 9." *CBQ* 76 (2014) 306–20.
Hagner, Donald A. *Matthew 1–3.* Word Bible Commentary. Dallas: Word, 1993.

Bibliography

Hardin, Justin K. "Galatians 1–2 without a Mirror: Reflections on Paul's Conflict with the Agitators." *Tyndale Bulletin* 65 (2014) 275–303.

Hartin, Patrick J. *James*. Sacra Pagina 14. Collegeville, MN: Liturgical, 2003.

Harvey, Irene E. "Exemplarity and the Origins of Legislation." In *Unruly Examples on the Rhetoric of Exemplarity*, edited by Alexander Gelley, 247–54. Stanford: Stanford University Press, 1995.

Hauser, Gerard A. "Aristotle's Example Revisited." *Philosophy and Rhetoric* 18 (1985) 171–80.

———. "The Example in Aristotle's Rhetoric: Bifurcation or Contradiction." *Philosophy and Rhetoric* 1 (1968) 78–90.

Hayes, Richard B. *The Faith of Jesus Christ: The Narrative Substructure of Galatians 3:1—4:11*. Grand Rapids: Eerdmans, 2002.

Hepburn, Brian, and Hanne Andersen. "Scientific Method." In *The Stanford Encyclopedia of Philosophy*, edited by Edward N. Zalta. https://plato.stanford.edu/archives/sum2016/entries/scientific-method/.

Hester, James D. "The Rhetorical Structure of Galatians 1:11—2:14." *Journal of Biblical Literature* 103 (1984) 223–33.

Holloway, Paul A. "The Enthymeme as an Element of Style in Paul." *Journal of Biblical Literature* 120 2 (2001) 329–43.

Holmberg, Bengt. *Paul and Power: The Structure of Authority in the Primitive Church as Reflected in the Pauline Epistles*. Philadelphia: Fortress, 1978.

Hughes, J. Donald. *Pan's Travail: Environmental Problems of the Ancient Greeks and Romans*. Baltimore: Johns Hopkins University Press, 1996.

Hultgren, Arland J. "Paul as Theologian: His Vocation and Its Significance for His Theology." *Word and World* 30 4 (2010) 357–70.

———. "Paul's Pre-Christian Persecution of the Church: Their Purpose, Locale, and Nature." *Journal of Biblical Literature* 95 (1976) 97–111.

Hunn, Debbie. "ΠΙΣΤΙΣ ΧΡΙΣΤΟΥ in Galatians 2:16: Clarification from 3:1–6." *Tyndale* Bulletin 571 (2006) 23–33.

———. "Pleasing God or Pleasing People? Defending the Gospel in Galatians 1–2." *Biblica* 91 (2010) 24–49.

Hurley, Patrick J. *A Concise Introduction to Logic*. 8th ed. Belmont,CA: Wadsworth, 2003.

Irwin, T. H. "Aristotle's Discovery of Metaphysics." *Review of Metaphysics* 31 (1977) 210–29.

Johnson, Alan F. "Assurance for Man: The Fallacy of Translating Anaideia by Persistence in Luke 11:5-8." *Journal of the Evangelical Theological Society* 22 (1979) 123–31.

Johnson, Curtis. "The Earth's Ethos, Logos, and Pathos: An Ecological Reading of Revelation." *Currents in Theology and Mission* 41 (2014) 119–27.

Josephus. *Complete Works*. Translated by William Whiston. Grand Rapids: Kregal, 1978.

Juza, Ryan P. "Echoes of Sodom and Gomorrah on the Day of the Lord: Intertextuality and Tradition in 2 Peter 3:7–13." *Bulletin for Biblical Research* 24 (2014) 227–45.

Bibliography

Kahl, Brigitte. *Galatians Re-imagined: Reading with the Eyes of the Vanquished.* Minneapolis: Augsburg Fortress, 2010.
King, R. A. H. *Aristotle and Plotinus on Memory.* Berlin: de Gruyter, 2009.
Kittel, Gerhard, and Gerhard Friedrich, eds. *Theological Dictionary of the New Testament.* 10 vols. Translated by G. F. Bromiley. Grand Rapids: Eerdmans, 1973.
Koptak, Paul E. "Rhetorical Identification in Paul's Autobiographical Narrative: Galatians 1:13—2:14." *Journal for the Study of the New Testament* 40 (1990) 97–113.
Kraftchick, Steven J. "Πάθη in Paul: The Emotional Logic of Original." In *Paul and Pathos,* edited by Thomas H. Olbricht and Jerry L. Sumney, 39–68. Atlanta: SBL, 2001.
Kraybill, Nelson J. *Apocalypse and Allegiance: Worship, Politics, and Devotion in the Book of Revelation.* Grand Rapids: Brazos, 2010.
Lane, Dermot A. *The Experience of God: An Invitation to Do Theology.* New York: Paulist, 2003.
Lategan, Bernard C. "Is Paul Defending his Apostleship in Galatians? The Function of Galatians 1.11–12 and 2.19–20 in the Development of Paul's Argument." *New Testament Studies* 34 (1988) 411–30.
———. "Paul's Use of History in Galatians: Some Remarks on His Style of Theological Argumentation." *Neotestamentica* 36 (2002) 121–30.
Leighton, Stephen R. "Aristotle and the Emotions." In *Aristotle's Rhetoric,* edited by Amélie Oksenberg Rorty, 206–37. Berkeley: University, 1996.
Leroi, Armand Marie. *The Lagoon: How Aristotle Invented Science.* New York: Viking, 2014.
Lesher, James H. "The Meaning of ΝΟΥΣ in the Posterior Analytics." *Phronesis* 18 (1973) 44–68.
Liubinskas, Susann. "Identification by Spirit Alone: Community Identity Construction in Galatians 3:19–14–7." *Asbury Journal* 67 (2012) 27–55.
Loubser, J. A. "The Contrast Slavery/Freedom as Persuasive Device in Galatians." *Neotestamentica* 28 (1994) 163–76.
Lyons, John D. *Exemplum: The Rhetoric of Example in Early Modern France and Italy.* Princeton: Princeton University Press, 1989.
Mack, Burton L. *Rhetoric and the New Testament.* Eugene, OR: Wipf & Stock, 1990.
Madden, James D. "Aristotle, Induction, and First Principles." *International Philosophical Quarterly* 44 (2004) 35–52.
Martin, Ralph P. *James.* Word Bible Commentary. Waco, TX: Word, 1988.
Martin, Troy W. "Apostasy to Paganism: The Rhetorical Stasis of the Galatian Controversy." *Journal of Biblical Literature* 114 (1995) 437–61.
———. "Invention and Arrangement in Recent Pauline Rhetorical Studies: A Survey of the Practices and the Problems." In *Paul and Rhetoric,* edited by J. Paul Sampley and Peter Lampe. New York: T. & T. Clark, 2010.
Martyn, J. Louis. *Galatians: A New Translation with Introduction and Commentary.* Anchor Bible 33. New York: Doubleday, 1997.

Bibliography

———. "A Law-Observant Mission to Gentiles." *Scottish Journal of Theology* 38 (1985) 307–24.
Matera, Frank. *2 Corinthians: A Commentary*. Edited by C. Clifton Black et al. Louisville: Westminster John Knox, 2003.
———. *Galatians*. Sacra Pagina. Collegeville, MN: Liturgical, 2007.
Milns, R. D. "Historical Paradigms in Demosthenes' Public Speeches." *Electronic Antiquity* 2 (March 1995).
Mitchell, Margaret M. *Paul and the Rhetoric of Reconciliation: An Exegetical Investigation of the Language and Composition of 1 Corinthians*. Louisville: Westminster John Knox, 1993.
Morris, Leon. *The Epistle to the Romans: The Pillar New Testament Commentary*. Grand Rapids: Eerdmans, 1988.
Moyise, Steve. "The Use of Analogy in Biblical Studies." *Anvil* 18 (2001) 33–42.
Murat, Aydede. "Aristotle on Episteme and Nous: The Posterior Analytics." *Southern Journal of Philosophy* 36 (1998) 1–48.
Nanos, Mark D., ed. "What Was at Stake in Peter's 'Eating with Gentiles' at Antioch?" In *The Galatians Debate: Contemporary Issues in Rhetorical and Historical Interpretation*, 282–318. Hendrickson, MA: Peabody, 2002.
Neuman, H. Terri. "Paul's Appeal to the Experience of the Spirit in Galatians 3:1–5: Christian Existence as Defined by the Cross and effected by the Spirit." *Journal of Pentecostal Theology* 9 (1996) 53–69.
Novak, Joseph A. "Socrates and Induction: An Aristotelian Evaluation." In *Shifting the Paradigm: Alternative Perspective on Induction*," edited by Paolo C. Biondi and Louis F. Groarke, 193–229. Boston: de Gruyter, 2014.
Oepke, Albrecht. *Der Brief des Paulus an die Galater, Theologischer Handkommentar zum Neuen Testament*. Edited by Joachim Rohde. Berlin: Evangelische Verlagsanstalt, 1973.
Papaioannou, Kim. "The Sin of the Angels in 2 Peter 2:4 and Jude 6." *JBL* 140 (2021) 391–408.
Polhill, John B. *Acts*. New American Commentary 26. Nashville: Broadman, 2001.
———. *Paul and His Letters*. Edited by Davis S. Dockery. Nashville: Broadman, 1999.
Pollock, John. *The Apostle: A Life of Paul*. Colorado Springs: Chariot Victor, 1985.
Price, Bennett, J. "Παραδειγμα and Exemplum in Ancient Rhetorical Theory." PhD diss., University of California at Berkley, 1975.
Quintilian. *Institutio Oratoria 1–3*. Translated by H. E. Butler. LCL. Cambridge: Harvard University Press, 1989.
Raisanen, Heikki. "Galatians 2:16 and Paul's Break with Judaism." *New Testament Studies* 31 (1985) 543–53.
Ramírez, Eduardo García. "Aristotle on Perception and Universals: An Extensional Reading." *Tópicos* 38 (2010) 49–84.
Reguero, M. Carmen Encinas. "Example and Similarity in Aristotle's Rhetoric." *Emerita* 85 (2017) 241–60.

Bibliography

Robinson, Donald William Bradley. "The Circumcision of Titus, and Paul's Liberty." *Australian Biblical Review* 12 (1964) 24–42.

Rogers, Cleon L., Jr., and Cleon Rogers III. *The New Linguistic and Exegetical Key to the Greek New Testament.* Grand Rapids: Zondervan, 1998.

Russell, Bertrand. *The Problems of Philosophy.* Amherst: Prometheus, 1988.

Russell, W. B. "Rhetorical Analysis of the Book of Galatians, Part 2." *Bibliotheca Sacra* 150 (93) 416–39.

Ryan, Eugene E. *Aristotle's Theory of Rhetorical Argumentation.* Montreal: Bellarmin, 1984.

Sanders, E. P. *Paul, the Law, and the Jewish People.* Minneapolis: Fortress, 1983.

Sanders, Jack T. "Paul's 'Autobiographical' Statements in Galatians." *Journal of Biblical Literature* 85 (1966) 335–43.

Schnelle, Udo. *Apostle Paul: His Life and Theology.* Translated by M. Eugene Boring. Grand Rapids: Eerdmans, 2005.

Schollmeier, Paul. "The Problem of Example." In *Shifting the Paradigm: Alternative Perspectives on Induction*, edited by Louis F. Groarke and Paolo C. Biondi, 231–50. Berlin: de Gruyter 2014.

Scola, Angela. "Christian Experience and Theology." *Library of Catholic Documents.* www.ewtn.com/library/Theology/EXTHEO.Htm.

Senior, Donald P., and Daniel J. Harrington, eds. *1 Peter, Jude and 2 Peter.* Sacra Pagina 15. Collegeville, MN: Liturgical, 2003.

Silva, Moises. "Abraham, Faith, and Works: Paul's use of Scripture in Galatians 3:6–14." *Westminster Theological Journal* 63 (2001) 251–67.

Sorabji, Richard. *Aristotle on Memory.* Chicago: University of Chicago Press, 2004.

Spicq, Ceslas. *Theological Lexicon of the New Testament.* Translated and edited by James D. Ernest. 3 vols. Peabody, MA: Hendrickson, 1994.

Stewart, Eric. "I'm Okay, You're Not Okay: Constancy of Character and Paul's Understanding of Change in His Own and Peter's Behaviour." *Hervormde Teologiese Studies* 67 (2011) 1–8.

Taylor, John W. "Demonstrating Transgression by Building Up the Faith: Argumentation in Galatians 2:17–18." *Bulletin for Biblical Research* 22 (2012) 547–62.

Taylor, N. H. "Paul's Apostolic Legitimacy, Autobiographical Reconstruction in Gal 1:11—2:14." *Journal of Theology for Southern Africa* 83 (1993) 65–77.

Thilly, Frank. *The Process of Inductive Inference.* Columbia: University of Missouri, 1904.

Tobin, Thomas H. *Paul's Rhetoric in Its Context: The Argument of Romans.* Peabody, MA: Hendrickson, 2004.

Tolmie, Francois Donald. "A Rhetorical Analysis of the Letter to the Galatians." PhD diss., University of the Free State, 2004.

Verseput, D. J. "Paul's Gentile Mission and the Jewish Christianity Community: A Study of the Narrative in Galatians 1 and 2." *New Testament Studies* 39 (1993) 36–58.

Vezina, Brad. "Universals and Particulars: Aristotle's Ontological Theory and Criticism of the Platonic Forms." *Undergraduate Review* 316 (2007) 101–3.

Bibliography

Vos, J. S. "Paul's Argumentation in Galatians 1–2." *Harvard Theological Review* 87 (1994) 1–16.
Walker, William O, Jr. "Why Paul Went to Jerusalem: The Interpretation of Galatians 2:1–5." *Catholic Biblical Quarterly* 54 (1992) 503–10.
Williams, Sam K. "Justification and the Spirit in Galatians." *Journal for the Study of the New Testament* 29 (1987) 91–100.
Wingate, Marc Gasser. "Aristotle on Induction and First Principles." *Philosopher's Imprint* (2016) 1–30.
———. "Aristotle on the Perception of Universals." Forthcoming—*BJHP*, 1–22.
Witherington, Ben, III. *The Acts of the Apostles: A Socio-Rhetorical Commentary*. Grand Rapids: Eerdmans, 1998.
———. *Conflict and Community in Corinth: A Socio-Rhetorical Commentary on 1 and 2 Corinthians*. Grand Rapids: Eerdmans, 1995.
———. *Grace in Galatia: A Commentary on Paul's Letter to the Galatians*. Grand Rapids: Eerdmans, 1998.

Ancient Documents Index

OLD TESTAMENT

Genesis

	48, 49, 113
1-2	6
3	48
6:1-4	48
7:16	48
8:16	48
12:1-5	111n66
13	111
15:1-5	111
15:1-16	111n66
15:6	45
15:6-22	44
17:1-19	111n66
18-20	49
18:1-33	111n66
22:17	111

Exodus

34	51

Joshua

2:8-13	44

1 Kings

18:19—19:3	60n59

2 Kings

9:7-37	60n59
9:30-37	61n61

2 Chronicles

24:20-22	55

Job

10	46n23
23	46n23

Psalms

37:25	27n11

Ancient Documents Index

Zechariah

55

DEUTEROCANONICAL BOOKS

1 Enoch

	47
1–36	48
10:8–10	48

ANCIENT JEWISH WRITERS

Josephus

63

Complete Works

| 486–90 | 11n11 |

Philo

63

NEW TESTAMENT

Matthew

1:19	58n52
6:25–34	26
6:26	26
6:27–32	26
6:28	26
7:7	35n25
16:21–23	31
17:4	25
23:3	39n3
23:35	55
27:45–54	24
27:54	24

Mark

| 6:14–29 | 56 |

Luke

1:1–3	36n28
7:19	23
7:22	23
10:25–37	61
11:5–8	53
24:13–35	30
24:32	31
24:33–35	32

John

| 8:12 | 58n54 |

Acts

	27, 77, 93, 99n35
2	30
5:1–11	58n52
9:1–19	32
9:2	102n38
9:4	101n37
9:26–28	108n58
9:26–30	93
10	103
10:1–8	29
10:9–16	29
10:17	29
10:19	29
10:24—11:18	30
10:28	30
11–14	71
11:25–26	109n58
11:29–30	93
11:30	109n58
13:2—14:28	109n58
14	71
15	93
16	71
16:3	102n38
18:23	93

Ancient Documents Index

20:35	38n3
22:3	78
22:4	101n37, 102n38
22:6–16	32n20
26:9–11	101n37
26:11	102n38
26:12–18	32n20

Romans

	45, 68n13, 79
3:27	77
4:3	45
5:12	79
5:13–20	80
5:20	79
6–7	80
6:14	79
7:1	39, 40
7:1–2	39
7:1–6	39, 40
7:2	39, 39n4
7:2–3	39, 40
7:4–6	40
8:28	35
16:25–26	116

1 Corinthians

	68n13
1:10	56
1:10–12	56n46
4:1	78n40
4:16	59n56
7–11	54
10:1–13	63
10:11	64
11:1	57n52
11:17–22	56
11:18	56
12:12–30	54
15:10	79n42

2 Corinthians

	68n13
1–10	79
3:14–15	51
3:15	51
6:2	35
11:22–29	34
12:1–10	33
12:7	33
12:9	79n42

Galatians

	67, 71, 115
1–2	45, 69, 70, 74
1	71, 93
1:1	68n9, 89, 109
1:1–12	68n9
1:6	66, 67, 68n9
1:6–9	52, 67, 67n8, 69, 74, 75, 85, 88, 100, 111, 112
1:7	68n9
1:7–8	78n40
1:8–9	87
1:9	68n9
1:10	69
1:10–12	52, 69, 74, 75, 85, 100, 109
1:11	68n9
1:11–12	68n10, 69, 89
1:12	69n14
1:13	101
1:13—2:14	72, 75
1:13–14	69, 70, 76
1:13–16	69, 70, 72, 75
1:13–17	69n14
1:13–24	69
1:15	79
1:15–16	69, 69n14, 70
1:17–20	75, 101n37
1:18	92

Ancient Documents Index

Galatians (cont.)

1:18–20	93
1:20	103
1:21	92
1:21—2:14	103
1:21–24	69, 72, 74, 75, 85, 88
1:23	101
1:24	91
2	93
2:1	92
2:1–10	68, 74, 75, 85, 92, 93
2:1–14	70, 88
2:2	93, 96
2:4	98
2:4–5	70, 96
2:5	95
2:6	96
2:7	99n35
2:7–8	98
2:7–10	109
2:9	99n35
2:10	96
2:11	100
2:11–14	29n16, 70, 71, 74, 75, 85, 99–100, 109
2:12	102
2:12–14	99n35
2:14	71, 72, 102
2:15	84
2:15–16	109
2:15–20	75
2:15–21	80
2:16	71, 80, 84
2:17–18	110
2:19–20	72
2:20	76, 109
2:21	79, 110
3–6	69, 72
3:1	84, 111
3:1–5	67, 75, 81, 83, 90, 116
3:2	83, 84, 112
3:2–5	82, 84n55
3:3	81, 83
3:4	81n49
3:5	84, 112
3:5–6	113
3:6	45, 112, 113
3:6–9	45, 75, 85, 110
3:8	83
3:14	84n55
3:14–18	113
3:14–23	83
3:26–29	115
4:1–7	82
4:6	84n55
4:8	112
4:8–11	67
4:12	72
4:12–20	76
4:16	109
4:21–31	51
5:1–2	87
5:2–3	116
5:6	116
5:7	81
5:7–10	67
5:8	81
5:10	76
5:11	101n38
6:2	77
6:12	102n38
6:17	76, 116

Ephesians

5:2	39n3

Philippians

	45, 68n13
3:17	59n56
4:9	59n56

Colossians

4:2	35

Ancient Documents Index

1 Thessalonians

	68n13
4:15	78n40

1 Timothy

1:15–16	58n52, 79
1:16	58n52
1:20	39n3

2 Timothy

1:15–18	58n52

Titus

1:11	39n3

Hebrews

10:19–39	43
11	43
11:1–2	43
11:1–3	35n26
11:3–40	43
11:6	35
11:31	44
12:1–2	39n3
12:1–13	43
12:3	39n3

James

2:14	43
2:14–17	43
2:14–26	43
2:15–17	44
2:18–20	44
2:18–25	43
2:21–23	44
2:21–26	43
2:25	44
2:26	43
4:3	35
5:11	46

2 Peter

	47
2:1–10	47
2:1–22	48
2:4	48
2:5–8	50
2:6	49
2:7	49
2:8	50
2:10a	49
3	48n29
3:4	36
3:6–7	36
3:9	36

1 John

	23
1:1	23
1:9	35
5:14	35

Jude

	47

Revelation

	27, 58n54, 64
2:13	55
2:20	59
2:22	60
2:23	61
9	65

Ancient Documents Index

GRECO-ROMAN LITERATURE

Aristotle 72

On Dreams

458b 9   130n36

On Memory and Recollection

	133n46, 134–36
1–2	136n51
2	137n56

Metaphysics

	123, 134
1.1.4–11	135n48
1.1.5–6	146n82
1.1.12	145n80
1.1.13	131n37
4.4.23	125n19
980a.1	123n8
981b.12	77n36

Nicomachean Ethics   77n36

On the Parts of Animals

3.2	130n35

Posterior Analytics

	140
1.1	8n1
1.12	77n37
1.18	124n14, 141n67
1.2	143n72
1.28	145n79
1.31	131n38, 132
2.2	131n40
2:19	140n64
2.14	135n49
2.19	132, 138nn60–61, 141n68
2.20	132n42

Prior Analytics

	10
1.30	145n79
2.23	9n5
2.24	9n2, 10n8

Prior and Posterior Analytics 129

Problems

18.3	73n26

Rhetoric

1/2/10–11	72n22
1.1.2	68n13
1.1.11	90n10
1.1.12	76n33
1.1.12–14	19n36
1.15.3, note a	88n7
1.2	105n48
1.2.19	15n23, 16n27, 17n32
1.3.5	18n35
1.3.9	14n21
1.4.9	83n52
1.6.1	18n34
1.9.40	17n33
2.1.8	105n47
2.20	12n12, 12n14, 74n29
2.20.3	12n16
2.20.8	45n18
3.16	64n71

Ancient Documents Index

Rhetoric to Alexander

	42
8	42n10
32.2	93n18

On Sleeping and Waking

455b 8	130n36

On the Soul

	123
2.6	123n12, 124n14, 125n20
2.9	124n14
3.2	126n23
5.4	124n14

Topics

	90n10
8.1	20n39, 62n65

Camillus, Marcus Furius	41–42
Choerilus	20n39
Cicero	57, 59, 91

De inventione

1.6	41n8

De Oratore

2.36.2.355	41n8

Orator

1.20.66	41n8

Pro Archia

14	41n8

Rhetorica ad Herennium

4.3.5	91n12

Tusculanae Disputationes

3.58	41n8

Demosthenes	85
Homer	20n39
Plato	19n37, 143–44
Pliny	57
Quintilian	52

Institutio Oratoria

12.4.1	52n39

Seneca	57
Socrates	134, 136, 146

www.ingramcontent.com/pod-product-compliance
Lightning Source LLC
Chambersburg PA
CBHW071502150426
43191CB00009B/1399